MACMILLAN MODERN DRAMATISTS

Macmillan Modern Dramatists

Series Editors: *Bruce King* and *Adele King*

Published titles

Eugene Benson, *J. M. Synge*

Renate Benson, *German Expressionist Drama*

Normand Berlin, *Eugene O'Neill*

Denis Calandra, *New German Dramatists*

Neil Carson, *Arthur Miller*

Ruby Cohn, *New American Dramatists, 1960–1980*

Bernard F. Dukore, *Harold Pinter*

Arthur Ganz, *George Bernard Shaw*

Frances Gray, *John Arden*

Julian Hilton, *Georg Büchner*

Charles Lyons, *Samuel Beckett*

Susan Bassnett-McGuire, *Luigi Pirandello*

Leonard C. Pronko, *Eugène Labiche and Georges Feydeau*

Jeannette L. Savona, *Jean Genet*

Theodore Shank, *American Alternative Theatre*

James Simmons, *Sean O'Casey*

David Thomas, *Henrik Ibsen*

Thomas Whitaker, *Tom Stoppard*

Nick Worrall, *Nikolai Gogol and Ivan Turgenev*

Katherine Worth, *Oscar Wilde*

Further titles in preparation

MACMILLAN MODERN DRAMATISTS

HENRIK IBSEN

David Thomas

Lecturer in Drama,
University of Bristol

MACMILLAN PRESS
LONDON

First published 1983 by
THE MACMILLAN PRESS LTD
London and Basingstoke
Companies and representatives throughout the world

ISBN 0 333 30595 7 (hc)
ISBN 0 333 30596 5 (pb)

Typeset by Wessex Typesetters Ltd
Frome, Somerset

Printed in Hong Kong

In memoriam T.B.T.

Contents

Contents

List of Plates

1. The tarantella scene, with Betty Hennings as Nora and Emil Poulsen as Torvald, in H. P. Holst's production of *A Doll's House*, Theatre Royal, Copenhagen, 1879. Teaterhistorisk Museum, Copenhagen.
2. William Bloch's promptbook notes for his production of *An Enemy of the People*, Theatre Royal, Copenhagen, 1883. Each character in the crowd scene is given a number, extra lines of dialogue are written in and blocking is shown in diagram form. Det kongelige Teaters bibliotek, Copenhagen.
3. André Antoine's production of *The Wild Duck*, Théâtre Libre, Paris, 1891. Contemporary sketch. University of Bristol Theatre collection.
4. Gordon Craig's production of *Rosmersholm*, Florence, 1906. University of Bristol Theatre Collection.
5. Design sketch by Edvard Munch for Max Reinhardt's production of *Ghosts*, Kammerspiele, Berlin, 1906. Munch Museum, Oslo.
6. Johanne Dybwad as Rebecca West in her own produc-

Editors' Preface

The *Macmillan Modern Dramatists* is an international series of introductions to major and significant nineteenth and twentieth century dramatists, movements and new forms of drama in Europe, Great Britain, America and new nations such as Nigeria and Trinidad. Besides new studies of great and influential dramatists of the past, the series includes volumes on contemporary authors, recent trends in the theatre and on many dramatists, such as writers of farce, who have created theatre 'classics' while being neglected by literary criticism. The volumes in the series devoted to individual dramatists include a biography, a survey of the plays, and detailed analysis of the most significant plays, along with discussion, where relevant, of the political, social, historical and theatrical context. The authors of the volumes, who are involved with theatre as playwrights, directors, actors, teachers and critics, are concerned with the plays as theatre and discuss such matters as performance, character interpretation and staging, along with themes and contexts.

BRUCE KING
ADELE KING

Acknowledgements

During the writing of this book, a number of individual people and institutions assisted and advised me, and I would like to record here my debt of gratitude to them. The staff of the Royal Library in Stockholm were particularly helpful, and at the University Library in Oslo, Øyvind Anker kindly offered advice on points of detail. I am indebted to Derek Russell Davis, Emeritus Professor of Mental Health at Bristol, for insights gained during our many discussions of the interactional patterns in Ibsen's work. I am most grateful to John Northam, Professor of Drama at Bristol, for ideas that bore fruit in Chapter 3. I am also most grateful to Dr Suzy Skevington of Bath University for commenting in detail on Chapter 4.

Finally, I would like to draw attention to the fact that some sections of my book are based on essays I have published elsewhere. Chapter 1 relates to my biographical essay on Ibsen in *Makers of Nineteenth-century Culture, 1800–1914*, edited by Justin Wintle, Routledge & Kegan Paul, 1982. My analyses of *Ghosts*, *Rosmersholm* and *When we dead awaken* relate in part to essays I have written for *Ibsenårbok* (1974), *Contemporary Approaches to Ibsen*, Vol. 4 (1979) and *Scandinavica* (1979).

A Note on Translations

Most of the quotations from Ibsen's plays are taken from the translations in *The Oxford Ibsen*. A reference in square brackets immediately following a quotation gives the appropriate volume number and page. Any translations that are not attributed in this way are my own.

1
Life and Work

Since his death in 1906, Ibsen has achieved the status of a modern classic. The impact of his work on twentieth-century theatre has been enormous. Directors have explored approaches to his plays ranging from the natural-ist to the expressionist, while playwrights as diverse as Harold Pinter and Arthur Miller have been influenced by his ideas. However, Ibsen often shocked and bewildered his contemporaries. The daunting complexity of his work baffled critics who were unwilling or unable to probe beneath the surface detail of his plays to seek out the patterns of meaning beneath the dialogue, the hidden poetry. He was accused of morbid pessimism by those who failed to recognise the life-affirming quality of his vision, despite the sombre tonality of his work. Modern criticism has led to a far clearer picture of the richness and subtlety of his writing; his plays have been explored from almost every conceivable critical starting point.

Ibsen often stressed the close relationship between his work and his life. In a letter to his German translator

Ludwig Passarge, written on 16 June 1880, he commented: 'Everything I have written has the closest possible connection with what I have lived through, even if it has not been my actual experience; every piece of writing has for me served the function of acting as a means of finding spiritual release and purification'. And yet many of the crucial experiences that helped to mould his consciousness and give shape and body to his work remain poorly documented. This is particularly true of the formative years he spent as a child in Norway. Throughout his creative life, and especially in his mature plays, Ibsen returned to the experiences of those early years. But we know tantalisingly little about them. Ibsen gave away very little in his letters, and comments by friends and relatives are few and far between. There is not even a portrait of his father and only a silhouette drawing remains of his mother. The bare facts of his early life can be summarised in a few paragraphs.

He was born in Skien in southern Norway on 20 March 1828. His father, Knud Ibsen, was a prosperous merchant who had married a wealthy young woman, Marichen, *née* Altenburg, in 1825. Ibsen's early years were spent in large houses filled with the sound of laughter and entertainment. By 1835, however, partly through unwise speculation and partly because of a general recession in trade, Knud's business empire collapsed; in order to pay off at least some of his creditors, he had to sell virtually all he owned, and the family was obliged to move out of town to Venstøp, a small country house he had bought in 1833. The feeling of social humiliation deeply affected the whole family, including Henrik, who was the oldest of Knud's and Marichen's five surviving children.

Until his confirmation in 1843, Ibsen lived at Venstøp, attending a secondary school in Skien. He was shy and introvert, but occasionally entertained his family with puppet shows of his own devising. Shortly after Christmas 1843, he was sent to Grimstad, a small coastal town some 100 km to the south, to earn his living as an apothecary's assistant. During his seven-year stay in Grimstad, Ibsen not only bore the major burden of running a busy apothecary's shop, he studied in the hope of preparing himself for university and wrote his first poems and his first play *Catiline* (*Catilina*, 1848–49). He fathered an illegitimate child by one of the maids who worked for the apothecary and had to pay paternity costs for the next fourteen years. In 1850 he left Grimstad for the capital city (it was then called Christiania), in order to attempt the university entrance examination. On the way to Christiania, he visited his parents. It was his first physical contact with them for seven years, and it was to be his last.

To fill in the details behind these bare facts, one has to resort to a combination of intelligent guessing and patient detective work. Overshadowing everything else were the family tensions that followed in the wake of Knud Ibsen's financial disgrace. Knud had refused to declare himself bankrupt, in order to retain his full rights as a citizen, but in consequence he remained weighed down by an enormous burden of debt for the rest of his life. His wife became bitter and introspective. The effect of these family tensions on the young Ibsen was deep and long lasting. He became almost aggressively shy and self-absorbed. His relationship with his father deteriorated. As Bergliot, his daughter-in-law, was later to comment: 'The relationship between father and son was not a very happy one. Henrik would remember even the smallest injustice . . .'[1]

Other evidence suggests that Ibsen's relationship with his mother was little better. There is no primary source describing that relationship while Ibsen lived at home. But we do know that he strongly disapproved of his mother's conversion to pietism in the late 1840s under the influence of a dissenting priest called Lammers. (Ibsen hinted as much in a letter to his uncle Christian Paus written in 1877 after the death of his father.) There is also the evidence of his plays and notes. There one finds the recurrent theme of an emotionally domineering mother who expects her son to compensate for the inadequacies of his father. In his notes for *The Wild Duck*, he described just such a mother in unflattering terms. The character is Old Ekdal's wife who was removed from *The Wild Duck* but reappeared later as Gunhild in *John Gabriel Borkman*: 'His vain wife. Half crazy as a result of the family's misfortunes. Herself partly to blame without realising it. Stupid idolatry of the son. Moaning and complaining' [vi, p. 431]. If this was, even partially, an image of how he saw his mother, it goes a long way towards explaining why, after his brief visit home in 1850, he never wrote to her or saw her again.

His years in Grimstad brought a series of different but no less important experiences. His brief sexual liaison with one of the apothecary's maids, ending with the birth of an illegitimate son, seems to have led to a life-long fear of eroticism and its consequences. Not surprisingly, many of his characters suffer, like their author, from the dual effects of erotic *angst* and thwarted sexuality.

In Grimstad, as he made his first literary experiments, a number of intellectual and spiritual experiences etched themselves deeply into his consciousness. He was particularly affected by the widespread social unrest in Europe during the year of revolutions in 1848 and by the growing conflict between Prussia and Denmark over Schleswig-Holstein. He described the influence of these events in some notes he wrote for the second edition of *Catiline* in 1875.

In these same notes he also picked out themes that seemed to him important for his later work: 'Much that my later work has dealt with – the conflict between aspiration and capacity, between will and ability, the overlapping of tragedy and comedy, whether on a general or an individual scale – is already mistily indicated here' [Meyer, p. 64]. Throughout his creative life, he himself felt the same clash between aspiration and capacity that he acknowledged here as one of the central themes of his work. Particularly in his early plays, his capacity to give expression to the complex human themes he wished to treat was severely limited by the Romantic, melodramatic form in which he was working. While his spirit soared, his intellect wrestled with a succession of intractable and unsuitable techniques. His apprenticeship as a writer was slow and painful, and at every stage he was beset by doubts.

In 1850, Ibsen left Grimstad for Christiania, determined to gain entry into university and equally determined to pursue a literary career. He did not achieve his first aim, failing the university's matriculation examination in two subjects (Greek and Mathematics) in August of 1850. But he largely succeeded in his second aim. Within months of his arrival in the capital, the Christiania Theatre had accepted his second play for performance; it was called *The Warrior's Barrow* (*Kæmpehøjen*) and was given its première on 26 September 1850. Written in a popular national-romantic style, it appealed to contemporary sensibilities and was surprisingly well received, in view of the complete lack of interest shown in his first play.

During the following year, he tried his hand at various forms of journalism, wrote a number of poems and became involved with a socialist workers' movement. When the police moved in to squash the movement and imprison its leaders in July 1851, Ibsen avoided arrest by pure chance. Fate was even kinder to him in October 1851, when it brought him into contact with Ole Bull, a virtuoso violinist

5

who was attempting to found a national theatre in his native town of Bergen. A concert was held in the capital to raise funds for the project, and Ibsen contributed some verses to this entertainment. Ole Bull was impressed by the verses and their author; as a result he offered Ibsen a job in his new theatre. The pay was meagre, but Ibsen accepted with alacrity. He was contracted to write at least one new play every year for the theatre and later was made stage manager and producer, responsible for the physical staging of new productions and for the characters' moves on stage.

In October 1851 Ibsen moved to Bergen. He stayed there for the next six years, experiencing the fleeting rewards and the many pitfalls of theatre life in a small provincial city. In 1852, his employers generously sent him on a study trip to visit theatres in Copenhagen and Dresden, but for the most part his work involved him in the routine drudgery of mounting a series of indifferent productions of even more indifferent plays in threadbare scenery and surroundings. His experiences undoubtedly gave him a solid theatrical grounding, which was invaluable to him in his work as a playwright, but they also left him with very mixed feelings towards the theatre. It was the start of a love-hate relationship that he never quite managed to resolve. In later life, he was eager to give practical advice on the casting and directing of his plays, but he was loath actually to set foot in a theatre to watch any of his plays in production.

The years at Bergen were difficult but not impossible; worse was to follow when Ibsen returned to Christiania in 1857 to become artistic director of the Christiania Norwegian Theatre. He began with high hopes, throwing himself into his new position with energy and enthusiasm. His career prospects had improved sufficiently for him to marry Suzannah Thoresen in 1858; she bore him a son called Sigurd in December 1859. For a while, things seemed to be going his way. But the financial position of the theatre was precarious and the public was fickle. Ibsen's plans for an ambitious repertoire were thwarted by a combination of public indifference and financial problems. Gradually he began to lose interest in his work, which provoked attacks on him from his own actors and from the press. He neglected his duties, began drinking heavily, and by 1862, when the theatre finally closed, was almost completely destitute. He even had to auction his possessions to meet unpaid tax demands. This was the absolute nadir of his career. For the next eighteen months he eked out a miserable existence as literary adviser to the rival Christiania Theatre. His application to Parliament in 1863 for a writer's grant was rejected. He was, however, given a small travel grant and this was augmented by public donations given in response to an appeal on his behalf, organised by his friend and rival Bjørnstjerne Bjørnson. In April 1864, Ibsen left Norway with his family. It was the start of an exile that was to last twenty-seven years.

During his years at Bergen and Christiania, Ibsen had written various poems and a steady flow of plays: *St John's Night* (*Sankthansnatten*, 1852); a revised version of *The Warrior's Barrow* (1854); *Lady Inger of Østråt* (*Fru Inger til Østråt*, 1855); *The Feast at Solhaug* (*Gildet på Solhaug*, 1856); *Olaf Liljekrans* (1857); *The Vikings at Helgeland* (*Hærmændene på Helgeland*, 1858); *Love's Comedy* (*Kærlighedens Komedie*, 1862); and *The Pretenders* (*Kongs-Emnerne*, 1863). In almost all of these plays, there were characters and themes that were to recur in his later work. But there was also a gulf, an incommensurateness between form and content. Romantic melodrama and the Scribean intrigue play proved to be an inadequate base from which to undertake a probing exploration of human aspirations and human interaction. They left little or no room for subtlety amidst the breathless detail of intrigue and plot. In his most successful play from the 1850s, for instance, *Lady Inger of Østråt*, the development of potentially interesting characterisation is consistently undermined by the melodramatic twists and turns of the complicated plot. Much the same can be said of *The Pretenders*, by far the most ambitious work of this early period. At moments it comes close to exploring in genuine human terms one of the central themes of his late work, namely the theme of vocation and its place within human experience. But there is no real balance in the play between the dynamics of the spiritual exploration and the remorseless pace of the complex Romantic intrigue.

Ibsen's poems from the 1850s and early 1860s take up similar themes to those explored in the plays. Generally, they suffer from Ibsen's all too quick facility for rhyming verse. The shape, the highly patterned structure of his verse forms inhibits the relaxed development of complex themes; as in the plays, there is a sense of the form and the feeling being at odds with one another. But in a few poems he manages to express precisely and succinctly crucial ideas that were to remain in the forefront of his consciousness as a creative writer. In *The Miner* (*Bergmanden*), for instance, written in 1851 and later revised for the collected edition of his poems in 1871, he expresses how he feels driven to explore the hidden depths of experience in his quest for insight. The imagery is muscular, the rhyming verse unusually discreet:

> Nej, i dybet må jeg ned;
> der er fred fra evighed.
> Bryd mig vejen, tunge hammer,
> til det dulgtes hjertekammer!

No, in the deep I must bore;
there is peace for evermore.
Break my way then, heavy hammer
to life's innermost secret chamber.

At the end of the 1850s, in his poem *On the heights* (*På vidderne*, 1859/60), he took up another important theme, exploring the clash he felt at the time between art and life. The poem is supposedly written by a young man who renounces the human ties represented by his fiancée and his mother in order to find 'freedom and God' up in the high mountains. (In this poem the high mountains symbolise man's striving to transcend himself through artistic endeavour; in Ibsen's later work they become more generally a symbol of man's desire for self-transcendence.) Even when he sees his mother's cottage in flames, a mysterious hunting companion shows him how to view the scene through his hollowed hand, 'for the sake of the perspective'. Despite the romantic trapping of the mysterious hunter and occasional examples of self-indulgent lushness in the verse, the poem is a vigorous and forceful statement of what was to become a persistent theme in Ibsen's plays from *Love's Comedy* to *When we dead awaken*.

When Ibsen left Norway for Rome in 1864, he initially travelled alone, leaving his wife and son in Copenhagen. The landscape, the architecture, the 'marvellously bright light which is the beauty of the South', the impact of new friendships, all had a liberating effect on him. He lived frugally on the small grant he had obtained (occasionally supplemented by further sums raised on his behalf by Bjørnson), frequenting the Scandinavian Club in Rome, and working assiduously on three projects: an epic poem called *Brand*, a prose drama called *Emperor and Galilean* and another epic poem on Norway. To begin with, he made slow progress on these projects, but by September 1865 the creative logjam had been released. What had suddenly come right for him was his work on the poetic drama *Brand*. In a letter to Bjørnson, he made it clear that his new work marked a complete break with the aestheticism of his poems and the national romantic themes of his earlier plays. He wrote *Brand* at furious speed in the summer of 1865. It was published in March 1866 and was an astonishing success. The turning point had come in his career as a writer.

In *Brand* the major character, who gives his name to the title, is a strong-willed country priest who demands that people give 'All or nothing' in their commitment to God. He refuses his mother absolution on her deathbed because of her greed for money. He also helps to cause the death of his wife Agnes by failing to understand her need to express grief when their child dies. At the end of the play, Brand finds that his insistence on total commitment has driven him away from human society. He is left wandering through snow-covered mountain peaks, alone and rejected. He dies in an avalanche, rebuked by the voice of God Himself. God is love, not the terrifying figure of Brand's imagination.

Brand was a play that challenged the religious and political orthodoxies of the contemporary world. It explored the demands and the limits of human will power, and posed a number of crucial questions for Ibsen and his readers. How can one fulfil oneself with a heritage of guilt? How does one reconcile will-power and a sense of vocation with love? How can one oppose the crass limitations of accepted social and political doctrines without being driven to extremes? *Brand* was a magnificent existential poem, sustained by a passionate belief in the possibility of conversion and redemption. Written in forceful rhyming verse, it was conceived as a literary drama and was not intended for the theatre (though it has proved to be an impressive work on the modern stage). As in Elizabethan drama, complex patterns of experience are fully communicated in the poetry. The poetry is the action. So far Ibsen had worked in a dramatic tradition where the theatrical devices or *coups de théâtre* were the action. He needed to make a complete break with this tradition in order to find himself as a dramatist.

Brand was followed within a year by *Peer Gynt* (1867), offering an exuberant treatment of a similar complex of themes. Structured like a morality play, it explored images of selfhood in a fanciful kaleidoscope of scenes; selfishness and selflessness are juxtaposed dialectically until the dialectical triad is resolved in the notion that 'to be oneself is to slay oneself'. Peer lives in a dream world of his own making. His life-long quest for self-fulfilment is in effect a continuous flight from self and from reality into a world of fantasy and fairy tale. In order to sustain this flight, Peer betrays principles and people – his mother; the bride he steals from her own wedding; Solvejg, the girl he loves. As the play progresses, he becomes more and more selfish. Only at the end, in a setting that strongly suggests a dream vision of purgatory, does he feel and experience the full horror of what he has done. The play closes with a pietà image in which Solvejg, his 'wife' and 'mother', cradles his head in her lap and claims that she has preserved his real self intact in her faith, her hope and her love. Written in cascading verse, *Peer Gynt* was effervescent and sparkling where *Brand* was steely and austere. But underneath the quite deliberate irony, it was a deeply serious play.

Its publication in November 1867 was eagerly awaited. A number of critics, however, particularly influential writers such as Clemens Petersen, were offended by the satiric barbs in the work and wrote disparagingly of it. Ibsen was furious and commented angrily in a letter to Bjørnson on 9 December 1867: 'My book is poetry; and if it isn't, it will become such. The conception of poetry in our country, in Norway, shall shape itself according to this book . . .'

In 1868 Ibsen moved with his family to Dresden; he was to remain in Germany for ten years, in order to ensure that his son had suitable schooling. There were still difficult years ahead of him, but from now on his social and financial position became increasingly stable. His income gradually permitted him to live comfortably if not luxuriously. As a sign of the distinction he had achieved, he was invited in 1868 to attend a prestigious nordic conference on orthography in Stockholm, where he made a favourable impression on King Charles XV. The king gave him the first of many medals that were to come his way (and Ibsen was to take a passionate delight in receiving honours and decorations); the king also saw to it that Ibsen was chosen to represent Norway at the opening of the Suez Canal in the autumn of 1869. This was a remarkable change in fortune. From the humiliations and defeats of the early 1860s, Ibsen had, by the end of the decade, acquired an international standing and reputation.

After settling in Germany, Ibsen devoted his attention to two main literary tasks. The first was to prepare a revised edition of his poems. This was published in 1871. It included both old and new material. Of the new material, arguably the most important was his *Rhymed Letter to Fru Heiberg* (*Rimbrev til fru Heiberg*) in which he reaffirmed his commitment to Romantic poetry:

> Prosa-stil er for ideer,
> vers for syner.

Sindets lyst og sindets veer,
sorg, som på mit hoved sneer,
harm, som lyner,
fyldigst liv jeg friest skænker
just i versets lænker.

Prose is for ideas and notions,
verse for visions.
The spirit's delight, the spirit's woe,
griefs falling on my head like snow,
anger's lightning blow,
to these I give life most freely
bound in the chains of poesy.

Ibsen wrote easily and spontaneously within the gentle
fetters of verse, but it gradually became clear to him that in
his work as a dramatist he must find a prose style that was
more in tune with the increasingly naturalistic temper of
the age. It was this second literary task that occupied most
of his creative energy during the 1870s. By sheer force of
will-power, Ibsen turned himself, during that decade, from
a Romantic poet into a master of naturalist prose dialogue.
But the transition was a slow and painful process.

It began in 1869 with a sparkling political comedy called
The League of Youth (*De Unges Forbund*), which was a
razor-sharp attack on the opportunism and empty rhetoric
of left-wing politicians in contemporary Norway. (At its
first production in Christiania, the play was met by a storm
of abuse from young radicals in the audience; it also led to a
distressing breach between Ibsen and his close friend
Bjørnson.) The plot, deriving from the well-made play
tradition of Scribe and Dumas *fils*, was unnecessarily
convoluted, but the major characters were convincingly
drawn as rounded individuals – notably the radical oppor-

tunist Steensgård and the caustic old cynic Daniel Hejre –
and the impression of provincial Norway (modelled on the
Skien of Ibsen's childhood) was persuasively realistic. One
of the minor characters in the play, Selma Brattsberg,
attracted the attention of the distinguished Danish critic
Georg Brandes, who commented in his review of the play
that she might well be used as a major figure in a later work.
Ten years later she reappeared as Nora in *A Doll's House*.

This was a promising beginning to Ibsen's search for an
acceptable approach to modern prose drama. His next
play, *Emperor and Galilean* (*Kejser og Galilæer*, 1873) was
more problematic. Written in two parts, it was conceived
ambitiously as a dramatisation of world-historical process,
offering 'a positive philosophy of life'.[2] The action was
anchored at a turning point of history, recording the waxing
and waning fortunes of Emperor Julian the Apostate
between AD 351 and 363. Julian was shown torn between
the demands of Christianity and the poetic but no longer
spontaneous beauties of paganism; his attempt to reconcile
the two in a Hegelian synthesis ends in complete failure.
There are naturalist features in the play: Julian's dilemma is
located in its historical context and the political and
ideological pressures affecting him are clearly set out.
Furthermore, the prose dialogue faithfully reflects the
speech patterns of real rather than idealised individuals.
Despite this, the overall texture of the work is epic and
Romantic, pointing back towards the verse plays *Brand*
and *Peer Gynt*. As in these two plays, *Emperor and
Galilean* was primarily concerned with one of the central
themes of Romanticism: the individual's quest for enlightenment.

Ibsen and some of his contemporaries regarded this play
as his masterpiece. The judgement of later critics has been
less enthusiastic. It does indeed have individual scenes that

are ruggedly powerful, but there is too much abstract philosophy and too little direct action to make the play theatrically effective. Nevertheless, the central vision it explores – the quest of the Emperor Julian for beauty and joy in life – was to remain of paramount importance in Ibsen's later work. Like Julian, many of Ibsen's later protagonists were to long for light and sunshine and pursue the same vision of beauty.

It was not until 1877, when he completed *Pillars of Society* (*Samfundets Støtter*), that Ibsen found a more relaxed approach to naturalist playwriting conventions. As in *The League of Youth*, he still relied on the well-made play archetype to provide the structural framework for the action, but there was a new assurance here in the way he handled theme, setting and characterisation. *Pillars of Society* was a witty and devastatingly accurate reckoning with the ruthless entrepreneurs who were spearheading the advance of industrial capitalism in contemporary Norway. The play offered a detailed and lively picture of life in a small Norwegian coastal town (almost certainly based on Grimstad), showing how easily such a community can be manipulated by its own pillars of the establishment, represented in the play by the figure of Consul Bernick. It was a sparkling piece, full of rounded characters whose speech was subtly differentiated. The play was a resounding theatrical success in Scandinavia and Germany, though it provoked a hostile response from critics in the Conservative press who had only a few years earlier been so delighted with *The League of Youth*. A contemporary cartoon showed Ibsen as the scourge of politicians of both the left and the right.

In 1878 Ibsen moved for a time to Rome before finally settling there again in the autumn of 1880. Almost at once he began making notes for what he called 'A modern tragedy': 'There are two kinds of moral law, two kinds of conscience, one in man and a completely different one in woman. They do not understand each other; but in matters of practical living the woman is judged by man's law, as if she were not a woman but a man' [v, p. 436]. The resulting play, *A Doll's House* (*Et Dukkehjem*, 1879), was a crushing indictment of contemporary bourgeois marriage.

Nora, the main character in the play, is first shown as a woman who revels in her status as the wife of a city bank manager, Torvald Helmer. The play builds to a crisis point when Helmer momentarily abuses and rejects his wife after learning that she once forged her signature in order to borrow to help save his life. From this central turning point, Nora sees her status in a totally different light, as that of a doll wife, a mere commodity to grace her husband's arm and bed. At the end of the play, she leaves her husband and her children to discover her real identity.

Initially, Ibsen uses an intrigue-play pattern to build a web of complications leading up to the central crisis. But instead of unravelling these in the second half of the play, the world of Nora and Helmer is exploded during their discussion of their motives and behaviour: the audience is left at the end with the broken fragments. This deliberate shattering of the conventions of the well-made play was as jarring to contemporary sensibility as Nora's decisive slamming of the door at the end of the play. Initially, the play was coolly received in the theatre, but its publication aroused widespread discussion and controversy. It was the play that was to make Ibsen internationally famous.

In his next play, *Ghosts* (*Gengangere*), written in Sorrento in 1881, Ibsen painted a sombre picture of what happens when a woman who has left her husband is forced by social pressure to return. Recapturing the analytic precision of classical Greek tragedy, the whole play is concerned with an extended exploration of past deeds in relation to the present. As layer after layer of the past is stripped away, Ibsen reveals the horrifying details of Mrs Alving's marriage, a marriage that has blighted the lives of husband and wife and their son Osvald. Ibsen shows how past and present deeds have forged a chain of events that leads inexorably to the madness of Mrs Alving's son Osvald. This was the play in which Ibsen achieved a final mastery of naturalist playwriting conventions. The social existence of the characters determines their consciousness; their environment shapes their patterns of behaviour. The dialogue is entirely dependent on characterisation, even when it meets the technical needs of exposition, plot and action. Even the retrospective structure is an expression of the theme (the effect of past deeds on the present), not just its vehicle. At last Ibsen had mastered what he was to call: 'The . . . difficult art of writing in the straightforward honest language of reality'.[3]

In many ways *Ghosts* marked a watershed in his career as a writer. He knew it would provoke a storm of abuse when it was published, but even he was shocked at the violence of contemporary responses to his play. In openly attacking the sanctity of marriage, Ibsen was threatening the very basis of patriarchal society and was duly vilified for his temerity. His initial reaction was to write an ironic riposte to his critics in the shape of a social comedy called *An Enemy of the People* (*En Folkefiende*, 1882). The major character, Dr Stockman, is hounded by members of his local community for attempting to publish details of the pollution affecting local bathing areas. The leaders of the community are concerned that such publicity would damage the commercial well-being of the town. Stockman is eventually muzzled, but even when a mob has broken the windows of his house, he still asserts defiantly that the strongest man is the one who stands alone. Stockman's lack of self-control and the exaggerated manner of his attack on official hypocrisy make his failure essentially comic. But underneath the laughter one can detect Ibsen's bitter resentment at the way he had been attacked by the 'compact majority' of right-thinking burghers. He was now aware, as he wrote in a letter to Sophie Adlersparre on 24 June 1882, that further than *Ghosts* he dare not go: 'A writer must not leave his people so far behind that there is no longer any understanding between them and him' [v, p. 477].

When he started work on his next play, *The Wild Duck* (*Vildanden*, 1884), he was at first still preoccupied with the way social existence determines consciousness. But as he settled down to work on the play, his passionate involvement with social and political issues mellowed. What emerged was a play concentrating on the politics of family life, showing how easily a fragile nexus of family relationships in the Ekdal home is shattered by the clumsy intervention of a neurotic outsider, Gregers Werle. As a result of the tensions created by Gregers's intervention in the marriage of Hjalmar and Gina Ekdal, Hedvig, their adolescent daughter, is driven to commit suicide in a gesture of sacrifice that is entirely pointless. There are numerous echoes in the play, in terms of character and setting, of Ibsen's own childhood experiences.[4] In its use of overt symbolism and its blending of tragi-comic effects, the play also marked a new, and for many a puzzling, departure.

In 1885 Ibsen moved from Rome to Munich. Before doing so, he visited Norway. It was a visit that prepared the way for his eventual return home to his native land in 1891. The immediate effect of the visit was to influence the mood and setting of his next two plays, *Rosmersholm* (1886) and *The Lady from the Sea* (*Fruen fra Havet*, 1888). Both plays are set in a small town in western Norway, clearly reminiscent of Molde where Ibsen spent two months in the summer of 1885. Both also explore complex states of mind, particularly in respect of the two main women characters, Rebecca West and Ellida Wangel.

In *Rosmersholm*, Rebecca West and her platonic lover, John Rosmer, act out a lethal drama of thwarted and diseased passion that ends with their suicide in the mill race. As they commit themselves to each other in a shared *Liebestod*, they also claim to be acting out a moral judgement on themselves for the part they have both played in the earlier suicide of Rosmer's wife Beate. But there is no certainty as to their real motives; the ending is deliberately ambiguous. There is an ironic juxtaposition between, on the one hand, the late romantic texture of the action and the symbolism and, on the other, the neo-classic precision of the play's analytic structure. Not surprisingly, *Rosmersholm* was met with complete bewilderment when it was first published. Even today its ambiguities can seem puzzlingly complex to actors and audiences.

The Lady from the Sea, by way of contrast, ends on a note of reconciliation, albeit tinged with sadness. The whole play is shot through with the symbolism of the sea, its changing state being reflected in the shifting moods of Ellida Wangel. Ellida is trapped in a debilitating marriage with a country doctor. Her longing for freedom and emotional fulfilment is encapsulated in the play in the figure of a mysterious seaman to whom she was once betrothed. He appears, as if conjured up out of the depths of her consciousness, to reclaim his bride. Confronted by this real or imaginary threat from her past, Ellida eventually chooses to commit herself freely to her husband and his two daughters from his previous marriage. The reconciliation is genuine, but the note of elegiac sadness in the ending is equally unmistakable. The sequences with the mysterious seaman have a dream-like quality foreshadowing the expressionist texture of Ibsen's late plays. *The Lady from the Sea* evoked a positive response from contemporary literary critics, but it proved less successful on stage. As with *Rosmersholm*, the complexity of imagery, symbolism and motivation proved difficult for actors and audiences to assimilate.

Ibsen had now reached another turning point in his life. His long years of exile had brought him fame and recognition. In 1891 he was to return home, an international celebrity, to the country he had left as a destitute failure in the early 1860s. In the meantime his son had grown up and entered the diplomatic service (he was also shortly to marry Bergliot Bjørnson, the daughter of Ibsen's great literary rival). He and his wife had lived together for more than thirty years in a relationship that was formal and respectful rather than warm and intimate. For twenty years he had worked in an orderly methodical fashion, publishing a new play every two years after a meticulous process of gestation, drafting and redrafting. In 1889, however, the ordered pattern of Ibsen's life was disturbed by a chance meeting on a summer holiday in Gossensass (now called Gardena).

It was there Ibsen met and became infatuated with an eighteen-year-old girl from Vienna called Emilie Bardach. From her portrait it is clear that she bore a striking resemblance to Ibsen's wife Suzannah as she was in her youth. Emilie represented all the promise and spontaneity of youth that Ibsen had long ago rejected in committing himself to the rigorous discipline of his artistic vocation. Eventually he broke with her. But further platonic affairs followed with young women in Munich and Christiania, with Helene Raff and Hildur Andersen. These experiences cruelly underlined the emotional sterility of his own respectable but loveless marriage and the emptiness of his formal, bourgeois life style. They marked the prelude to the final phase of his career as a playwright. From this point onwards, his plays reflect an increasingly icy soulscape in which images of frustration, failure, impotence and stunted potential assume an ever more dominant role.

In *Hedda Gabler* (1890), the major character is a general's daughter who finds herself trapped in a conventional bourgeois marriage with a dull academic husband. Various threats confront her during the play. The threat of social *déclassement* if her husband fails to obtain the professorial appointment promised him; an emotional threat from her past in the shape of Ejlert Løvborg, a man she once loved though too cowardly to admit it; the threat of sexual blackmail from Judge Brack. The play ends with Hedda's suicide, the only gesture she can find that adequately expresses her contempt for the sordid limitations she sees all around her. Despite the seriousness of the theme, a strong sense of black comedy runs through the action. In *The Wild Duck*, the mingling of tragi-comic effects was gentle and ironic; here it is cruel and savage, almost bordering on the absurdity of farce. Ibsen's contemporaries were outraged. The play was almost universally condemned.

After moving home to Norway in 1891, Ibsen embarked on a series of plays that culminated in what he himself called his dramatic epilogue, *When we dead awaken*. All of them make extensive use of verbal and visual symbolism; all of them have at times an almost dream-play quality that points towards the drama of expressionism; increasingly, the structural patterns tend towards the kaleidoscopic mingling of past and present. In their different ways, they constitute Ibsen's final searing judgement on himself as a man and an artist and on the materialistic values of the world in which he had lived and worked.

In *The Master Builder* (*Bygmester Solness*, 1892), Solness the main character fears the threat of youth. His life and marriage seem to him empty and pointless; the only way he can survive is by ruthlessly exploiting the young people who work for him. The sterile order of his world is eventually upset by the arrival of a young woman admirer called Hilde. The parallel with Ibsen's own life is quite clear. But where Ibsen withdrew from his relationship with Emilie Bardach before it destroyed his peace of mind, Solness is driven by Hilde to prove his virile creativity in attempting to climb the high tower he himself has designed. He falls to his death and, in so doing, expresses something of Ibsen's fears of artistic and personal impotence.

Little Eyolf (*Lille Eyolf*, 1894) is dominated by themes of vibrant but thwarted eroticism. Much of the play explores a sustained incestuous fantasy involving Asta and her supposed half-brother Alfred Allmers. By the end of the play, it is only in renouncing overt sexuality that the main characters can achieve any form of mental and spiritual equilibrium. The calm at the end of the play is not so much the calm of reconciliation as the icy calm of death as Allmers and his wife Rita look: 'Up towards the mountain peaks. Towards the stars. Towards the vast silence'.

John Gabriel Borkman (1896) is set in a winter landscape both physically and spiritually. Borkman is a former industrial magnate who overreached himself and had to serve a lengthy prison sentence for speculating with money and shares belonging to others. He also ruthlessly sacrificed the woman he loved for the sake of personal ambition, for the power and the glory. Borkman now lives like a caged wolf, never meeting, never speaking to his embittered wife,

Gunhild, who cannot forgive him for the shame he has brought on them. At the end of the play, their son Erhart has fled from them to live his own life and Borkman dies in the icy wastes, still dreaming of the power and the glory. Painful memories of Ibsen's childhood, blended with more recent experiences from his marriage, underpin this final reckoning with the destructive values of contemporary bourgeois society. The play can also be read as an oblique criticism of Ibsen's commitment to art in preference to a life of emotional fulfilment.

Finally, in *When we dead awaken* (*Når vi døde vågner*, 1899), Ibsen returned yet again to the clash of art and life, vocation and personal happiness. It was a recurrent theme that had preoccupied him throughout his creative life. An ageing sculptor Rubek is confronted by Irene, the woman who was his youthful inspiration but whom he rejected for the sake of artistic and material advancement. He now discovers that what he lost in rejecting her was the only thing that matters in life: the ability to face himself and to respond to others with complete authenticity. It is too late to live his life again, but in the final scene of the play, acted out on the mountain peaks, he commits himself to Irene irrevocably, passionately in a *Liebestod* that achieves mythical stature. In this dramatic epilogue Ibsen guides us through a dream-like spiritual landscape, expressionistically blending myth and reality.

These late plays required a style of acting and presentation that the contemporary theatre was ill-equipped to meet. Gifted critics such as James Joyce and George Bernard Shaw responded warmly to their subtlety, but in general they were politely rather than enthusiastically received.

On 5 March 1900, Ibsen wrote to Moritz Prozor: 'If it be granted to me to retain the strength of body and spirit

23

which I still enjoy, I shall not be able to absent myself long from the old battlefields. But if I return, I shall come forward with new weapons, and with new equipment' [Meyer, p. 829]. Whatever new projects were in his mind, his hopes of retaining his strength of body and spirit were soon dashed. On 15 March he suffered a stroke, which left him unable to write. A year later he suffered a further stroke. He lived another five years, dying on 23 May 1906. His countrymen, whose scorn for his early work had once driven him into exile, honoured him with a state funeral.

2
Literary and Theatrical Influences

Norway, in the nineteenth century, faced the task of developing a national identity in politics, literature and the theatre. Until the Napoleonic wars, Norway had been ruled for four hundred years by Denmark; its cultural and social life was accordingly dominated by Danish example. After 1814, when Swedish troops crossed the border and imposed a political union on Norway, the struggle for political independence was directed against the Swedish crown. However, Denmark retained its dominant influence over Norwegian literature, theatre and language. Early in the century, writers were completely dependent upon Danish tastes, even to the extent of using a language whose grammar and orthography were almost indistinguishable from Danish. By the end of the century, a recognisably Norwegian body of literature had been written, a strong Norwegian theatre had been established and language reforms had helped to create a modern Norwegian language that was distinct from Danish. (Norway is still beset by language problems that date from the nineteenth century, with the Western part of the country claiming that its form of Norwegian known as 'nynorsk' is more genuinely Norwegian than the Danish inspired 'riksmål' of the Eastern provinces.)

Ibsen played a crucial role in establishing Norway's cultural identity, both as a dramatist and a man of the theatre. Inevitably, however, his early work was influenced and even moulded by Danish example.

By the beginning of the nineteenth century there were flourishing amateur dramatic societies in most important Norwegian towns. However, professional theatre was firmly in the hands of Danish players, both in the capital – in the Christiania Theatre (founded in 1827) – and in the provinces, where troupes of Danish actors toured on a circuit basis. Ibsen's earliest experiences of the theatre were accordingly at performances of one of the four touring Danish companies that visited Skien during the 1830s and 1840s. The repertoire of these touring companies consisted of a mixture of French and Danish vaudevilles, light social comedies and romantic melodramas. The standards of acting and production were primitive, and facilities for audiences and actors were basic (there was, for instance, no heating during the winter).

Ibsen makes no direct mention of any early theatre visits in his letters or biographical notes, but he does refer warmly and affectionately in *Pillars of Society* to the gaiety of the amateur drama societies in the early years of the century. He also mentions the impact made by a Danish touring company when it visited the small coastal town in which the play is set:

MRS RUMMEL: Well, you see . . . that was the winter
Møller's theatrical company was in town . . .

MRS HOLT: . . . And among the actors in the company was
a man called Dorf, together with his wife. All the
young men fell for her completely.   [v, p. 33]

It is no coincidence that one of the companies that visited
Skien was led by a man called J. P. Miller.

Another influence on Ibsen's early development as a
writer was the work of the Danish writer Adam
Oehlenschläger, whose romantic tragedies Ibsen read
during his apprenticeship in Grimstad. His first play,
Catiline, tracing out the abortive conspiracy and rebellion
of Catiline against the Roman Senate, shows signs of
Oehlenschläger's influence in its language, its exotic historical setting and the highly charged romantic atmosphere of
individual scenes (many of which take place in darkness or
moonlight, with claps of thunder punctuating the action at
its climax). His second play, *The Warrior's Barrow*, is even
more clearly indebted to Oehlenschläger's work in its
choice of theme (the struggle between pagan values and
Christianity) and in its Viking setting.

After moving to the capital in 1850, Ibsen was given a
free pass for the Christiania Theatre when his play *The
Warrior's Barrow* was accepted for performance. He also
wrote a number of reviews for a weekly magazine he
published with two friends, Paul Botten Hansen and A. O.
Vinje. These early reviews show his warm liking for
romantic opera, suggest a certain ironic disapproval
of 'Scribe & Co's sugar-candy dramas' [i, p. 601], and
show Ibsen's exasperation with the naïvety and cultural
obtuseness of contemporary audiences. The latter
point was to remain a constant leitmotiv in the reviews he
wrote during the 1850s and early 1860s. Another feature

he was to stress was the importance of establishing a distinctly Norwegian theatre tradition, free from Danish influence.

Initially, however, it was Danish and German theatre practice that determined the parameters within which he took his first hesitant steps as a stage manager and producer. When he joined the company of The Norwegian Theatre in Bergen in October 1851, he was engaged as a resident playwright and was expected to produce a new play for the theatre every year. The management had already appointed Herman Laading as 'artistic director' but now gave some thought as to how these two men might profitably work together. The solution they proposed in February 1852 was based on the ideas of Heinrich Laube, artistic director of the Burgtheater in Vienna. Laading was to be given responsibility for the theoretical aspect of each production (the interpretation of the play and the individual roles), while Ibsen was made responsible for the practical execution (the moves and gestures on stage and the overall stage setting).

To prepare Ibsen for his new task, the Board of Management gave him a travel grant to visit two of Europe's leading theatres: The Theatre Royal in Copenhagen and The Royal Court Theatre in Dresden. Copenhagen's Theatre Royal (Det kongelige Teater) had at its disposal in 1852 one of the finest acting ensembles in the whole of Europe. It offered (as it still does today) plays, opera and ballet in repertoire. It was controlled by a gifted artistic director, J. L. Heiberg, who was at the zenith of his career. Ibsen was warmly received and impressed by what he saw. An immediate and tangible result of his visit was the acquisition of play scripts, musical scores and books on costuming. He also learnt how to keep a promptbook, containing floor plans, lists of scenery, furniture and props and with diagrams for the moves and positions of the actors. Less tangible, but no less important was the impact on Ibsen of Heiberg's aesthetic ideas and the deep impression made on him by the acting of Heiberg's wife, Johanne Louise Heiberg.

Heiberg was a playwright, philosopher and critic, as well as a man of the theatre. After a visit to Paris in the 1820s, he had set himself the task of introducing the wit, elegance and laughter of modern French culture into the Danish theatre. He began his campaign in 1825 with a successful production of his vaudeville called *King Solomon and George the Hatter* (*Kong Salomon og Jørgen Hattemager*). He followed up this success with further vaudevilles and with translations of modern French plays, including sixteen written by Scribe. He also wrote a spirited vindication of his approach in an essay entitled *On the Vaudeville as a dramatic form* (1826). The effect of Heiberg's three-fold strategy was to banish from the repertoire of The Theatre Royal the romantic melodramas of Iffland and Kotzebue and open the way for the plays of Scribe and, more importantly, for a specifically Danish form of *Biedermeier* romantic drama, offering its audiences a combination of charm, wit, irony and song.

Heiberg's example was followed by other authors, the most famous of whom were Henrik Hertz and Jens Hostrup. Already by the late 1820s and early 1830s, however, Heiberg felt there was a danger of the vaudeville becoming altogether too prosaic. In order to provide an artistic counterbalance for public taste he wrote in 1828 his romantic ballad play, *The Fairy Hillock* (*Elverhøj*), and in 1835 a romantic fairy-tale comedy called *The Elves* (*Alferne*), both of which proved to be as successful as his vaudevilles. In this conscious attempt to balance in his work the everyday and the romantic, Heiberg remained faithful to the Hegelian notion of reconciling conflicting opposites within himself.

The same was true of his wife's acting. Johanne Louise Heiberg was the leading actress of her day. She personified the blending of impassioned romanticism with the idealised beauty of *empire* neo-classicism. Her acting style was characterised by a graceful, sculptured quality in movements and positions. At the same time, she delighted in portraying exotic and complex characters. In her youth, she was best known for her acting of coquettish ingénues. By the time Ibsen saw her, she was a distinguished character actress famous for her command of picturesque mime and dumb show and for her ability to convey both the innocent and the sensual, the naïve and the passionate. The impression she made on Ibsen was vivid and long-lasting. Twenty years later he recalled it in his poem *Rhymed Letter to Fru Heiberg* (*Rimbrev til fru Heiberg*, 1871):

> mindet om en skønhedsfyldig
> > højtids-stund,
> mindet om en rad af timer,
> > langt tilbage,
> da jeg så Dem sejrrig drage
> smykket, gratie-fulgt og sand
> gennem kunstens under-land.

> The memory of a beauty-laden
> > Festive moment,
> The memory of a string of hours,
> > Lost in time,
> When first I saw you glide victoriously sublime,
> Bejewelled, with grace and truth of heart,
> Through the wonderland of art.

The tragic heroines he created during the 1850s, Lady

Inger in *Lady Inger of Østråt* and Hjørdis in *The Vikings at Helgeland*, are clearly written with the acting style of Fru Heiberg in mind. Both are complex characters attempting to reconcile powerfully conflicting emotions. Even a later tragic heroine like Hedda Gabler, torn between irreconcilable responses, is conceived in a similar manner. Indeed much of what happens to Hedda is prefigured in the deeds and responses of Hjørdis.

Another important experience in Copenhagen was Ibsen's discovery of an influential work on dramatic theory and playwriting: Hermann Hettner's *Modern Drama (Das moderne Drama)*. Hettner argued for the primacy of psychological conflict in drama and suggested that even in historical tragedies, it was important to provide a detailed psychological basis for character drawing. It was not the historical events that mattered but the clash of wills; it was this aspect that contemporary audiences would appreciate. Hettner also went on to write about fairy-tale comedies as a genre and suggested that the important thing was the juxtaposition of the worlds of everyday reality and fantasy. These were ideas that Ibsen was to follow in the historical dramas and ballads or fairy-tale plays he wrote during the 1850s.

When Ibsen returned to Bergen in July 1852 after his four-month tour to Copenhagen and Dresden, his mind was full of stimulating impressions and memories, and these bore fruit in his playwriting. His fairy-tale comedy, *St John's Night*, was directly influenced by Heiberg's example. Even Heiberg's repertoire policy was reflected in the choice of plays performed at Bergen during the 1850s. Above all, however, Heiberg's advocacy of modern French theatre contributed to Ibsen's renewed respect for Scribean playwriting techniques. His historical plays written at Bergen show clear signs of Scribe's influence.

31

In *Lady Inger of Østråt*, for instance, the complex plot with its sudden reversals and delayed revelations is based on Scribean example, as is the way Ibsen blends together the private and public worlds of the major characters, Lady Inger and the Danish knight, Nils Lykke. The play is set in Norway in 1582 at a time when the Danes were attempting to crush the Norwegian nobility. Lady Inger plays a dangerous game of double bluff, poised between her own countrymen and the Danish oppressors. But her real motives are personal rather than patriotic. She has fought for twenty years to safeguard the future of her illegitimate son whom she wants to be king of Norway. To that end, she has sacrificed her own and her daughters' happiness. She even stoops to murder, only to discover too late that her victim is her son whom she has not seen since his birth.

On this Scribean framework, Ibsen built a romantic melodrama that bears his own unmistakable imprint. Two features above all distinguish the play from Scribe's historical works. The first is Ibsen's attempt to explore Lady Inger's complex and anguished state of mind. This culminates in Act 5 in a scene where her spiritual torment at the murder she has ordered is reminiscent of Lady Macbeth's. The second is Ibsen's confident use of romantic visual devices in the stage setting. The action takes place in and around the Great Hall at Østråt. The scenery and lighting effects suggest a dominant mood for each act, progressing from the mystery and confusion of Act 1, with a moonlit upstage area, a glowing fire downstage and a noisy storm outside, to the spiritual anguish of Act 5 where the darkness surrounding Lady Inger is broken only by one lighted candelabra on a table. In a way that foreshadows Mrs Alving's attempt to dispel Osvald's doubts and uncertainties in Act 2 of *Ghosts* by asking for the lamp to be lit, Lady Inger attempts equally vainly to calm her racing thoughts at the end of Act 5 by calling for more candelabras to be lit. Already here, Ibsen uses stage and lighting effects to convey to an audience the inner, spiritual state of mind of his characters.

During the seven years he worked in Bergen, Ibsen was responsible for some sixty-seven productions. Contemporary audiences demanded a rapidly changing repertoire, which left little time for subtlety of either acting or directing. New productions were given no more than five or six rehearsals before they opened. The casting was in the hands of the Board of Management, although both Laading and Ibsen could make their own suggestions. The initial read-through was supervised by Laading, whose task it was to give notes on the interpretation of the play and the individual characters. The actors were then required to learn their parts by heart. The remaining rehearsals were blocking rehearsals, with the function of establishing the moves of the characters, their entries and exits and the general use of stage space. These were supervised by Ibsen, though Laading had the right to intervene.

Ibsen prepared careful notes and diagrams in his prompt-books for placing the actors on the stage. Inevitably, the conventional neo-classic format of actors grouped in a half-circle around the prompter's box (downstage centre) can be found in his notes. But what is far more interesting is his attempt to break away from this in some of his settings and to introduce less symmetrical, rather more picturesque uses of the stage space in terms of the characters' moves and the placing of furniture.[1] He used a system of numbers and dotted lines to indicate the position and moves of different characters on stage. From this it is clear that he envisaged a strongly visual, romantic production style, where the actors contributed through tableaux and blocking, often in upstage positions, to the overall picturesque effect of the play (as opposed to the neo-classic style where attention was focused on the rhetorical exchanges of the actors who were placed downstage and seen against, rather than within, a pictorial framework).

The stage at Bergen, with its sloping floor and pairs of receding wings, with its painted backcloths and borders, its oil lamps and candles, was essentially the Baroque stage of the eighteenth century. Laading still favoured a neo-classic declamatory style that was perfectly in keeping with this stage environment.[2] Ibsen, on the other hand, seems to have favoured a move towards a more colourful and romantic use of the stage space, with visually effective groupings and moves and, in his own plays, exotic historical or fantasy settings.

Some contemporary reviews suggest that Ibsen's theatre work was often warmly received, particularly in the first season when he spent a great deal of time preparing his *mises en scène*.[3] But his relationships with his colleagues were often difficult (actors trained in the stock moves, gestures and declamation of the neo-classic theatre resented the intrusion of a director), and there were too many limitations imposed on his creativity by the Board of Management. In addition, only one of the five plays he had written at Bergen – *The Feast at Solhaug* – had enjoyed any success in production. In August 1857, he was released from his contract at Bergen and moved to Christiania to take up a new post as artistic director of the Norwegian Theatre (founded in 1852 in emulation of Bergen's Norwegian Theatre).

Despite the disappointments and frustrations he experienced during his stay in Bergen, Ibsen had learnt a number of important lessons whose influence can be detected even in his mature plays. His work on the visual aspects of production – movement, gesture, placing, setting – gave him a clear grasp of the expressive possibilities of the Romantic theatre, with its scope for adding visually poetic resonances and shades of meaning to prose dialogue. This was a technique he was to exploit again and again in the prose plays of his maturity, where subtly changing lighting states and romantic visual symbols (for instance, Rebecca's white shawl in *Rosmersholm* or the mysterious loft in *The Wild Duck*) add extra layers of meaning to the dialogue. Another lesson he never forgot was the importance of expressive entrances and exits. Drawing on the experiences he gained in Bergen, Ibsen meticulously suggests in the stage directions of his later prose plays dominant upstage entries for the first appearance on stage of key figures in the action (for instance, Osvald's first entry in *Ghosts* or Hedda's first entry in *Hedda Gabler*) and always provides visually expressive exits at crucial moments (Nora's slamming of the door at the end of *A Doll's House* or Ulrik Brendel's cryptically threatening exit in the last act of *Rosmersholm*). Even his liking for picturesque tableaux is reflected, albeit ironically, in the later plays (Bernick surrounded by admiring women at the end of *Pillars of Society*, or Osvald slumped in his chair at the end of *Ghosts*, with his mother standing behind him). In all his late plays, including his ostensibly naturalist plays, Ibsen exploited the visual techniques of the romantic theatre that he had tested out in his productions at Bergen.

In moving to Christiania to take up the position of artistic director of The Norwegian Theatre, he had high hopes of making a decisive contribution to the development of a specifically Norwegian theatre style, free from Danish influence. His aim was to develop a national romantic repertoire that would express the unique quality of Norwegian cultural life and traditions. But underneath this nationalist commitment, one can still detect the influence of Heiberg's demand for ideal truth in art.

In the first year of his appointment, Ibsen approached this new challenge with creative vigour and polemic verve. (The acidity of his newspaper articles made him many enemies.) However, his plans were entirely frustrated by the economic and human limitations of the Christiania Norwegian Theatre. The theatre was already burdened with debt when he took it over. In addition, it was situated in a poor quarter of town and attracted audiences with neither taste nor discernment. Much to his chagrin, Ibsen found that his actors were unable to meet the artistic demands he made of them and his audiences were more interested in mindless escapism than a programme of national romantic theatre. In the spring of 1859, for instance, his own play *Lady Inger of Østråt* had to be removed from the repertoire after only two performances to make way for a pair of English dancers who filled the house night after night.

By 1860 it was clear to Ibsen that his programme had failed. The rival Christiania Theatre with its Danish actors remained the leading theatre in town. His attempts to introduce serious Norwegian plays into the repertoire had led to a series of box-office disasters. The only recourse left to him was to import the escapist farces from Copenhagen that his audiences wanted. At this point, Ibsen lost interest in the theatre and began neglecting his duties. The remaining two years until the theatre went bankrupt were among the most humiliating he ever spent.

One of the unfortunate side-effects of the unhappy years he spent running The Norwegian Theatre in Christiania was the way it drained his creative energy as a writer. During the five years when he was artistic director of the theatre, he did not manage to complete a single play. Only after the collapse of the theatre in 1862 did he gradually rediscover the creative verve he had lost in administering an ailing theatrical enterprise.

A study trip to the fjords in Western Norway in the summer of 1862, financed by a government grant, gave him the breathing space he needed to complete his play *Love's Comedy*. Written in almost epigrammatic verse, it was a witty and polished affirmation of romantic aestheticism (of the kind he had first encountered in Denmark in 1852) in preference to bourgeois domesticity. It was by far the best play he had so far written, even if, with its highly patterned verse form, its overall feel was more literary than theatrical. Its worldly theme and ironically sophisticated tone shocked the narrow-mindedly provincial critics of contemporary Norway.

In writing his next play *The Pretenders* in 1864, Ibsen returned to the theme of national romanticism that had underpinned his best practical theatre work. The play traces out the rivalry between Håkon Håkonssøn and Earl Skule for the throne of Norway, culminating in the death of Skule and the decisive victory of Håkon who is fired with the kingly thought that: 'Norway has been a kingdom; it shall become a people'. *The Pretenders* was a self-confident expression of the various national romantic values that had inspired Ibsen's work throughout the 1850s. It was written in a way that brought together the various sources of inspiration on which he had drawn since his stay in Copenhagen in 1852. Structurally, the play uses a well-crafted, Scribean intrigue-play pattern, but it far surpasses, in its epic sweep, anything Scribe wrote in his historical dramas. In its detailed study of complex individuals – the assured leader Håkon, the self-doubting Skule, and the scheming Bishop Nikolas – it fulfils all the demands that Hettner had outlined in respect of modern historical drama. What makes the play particularly impressive is the way Ibsen turned all the defeats and failures of the 1850s and early 1860s into a triumphal assertion of the national romantic theatricality he had consistently advocated.

Imposing Gothic settings dominate the stage as the action moves from thirteenth-century Bergen to Oslo and finally to the medieval coronation town of Nidaros. Church portals and palace interiors provide a visually impressive backcloth to Ibsen's exploration of political jealousy and intrigue at a crucial point in Norway's history. There are colourful crowd scenes, tableaux and even a full-scale battle on stage as Håkon and Skule, flanked by their respective supporters, vie for the crown. Processions of monks and priests with censers and banners punctuate the action as a visual reminder of Bishop Nikolas's brooding presence. Even after his death, his baleful influence is signified by a red comet seen shining in the sky as his ghost appears to tempt Skule to further crimes of treason. At several points in the action, Ibsen uses the atmospheric lighting effects of his earlier plays. But the most striking feature of *The Pretenders* is its pageantry and visual splendour as Ibsen underlines in stage terms the serious-ness and dignity of its national theme, tracing Norway's development from a kingdom to a nation.

Ibsen was invited to direct the first production of the play in January 1864 at the Christiania Theatre which, following the demise of the rival theatre in 1862, had acquired Norwegian actors. The result was a personal and artistic triumph, fulfilling all the aims Ibsen had set himself in his theatre work. The audience responded enthusiastically to the play and Ibsen was called on to the stage after the final curtain to be greeted by tumultuous applause. At last he had shown that a genuinely Norwegian romantic theatre was indeed viable.

This was to be his swan song in the theatre. He had already completed his plans for leaving Norway. In April of that year he set out for Copenhagen on the first stage of the journey that was to take him into exile in Italy. In future his only practical contact with the theatre was to be limited to making suggestions about casting or staging his own plays. But at least he had the satisfaction of making a triumphant exit from a profession that had often brought him disappointment and humiliation.

3
Philosophical and Aesthetic Ideas

Ibsen's major poetic dramas, *Brand* and *Peer Gynt*, were born of indignation. Denmark's humiliating defeat at the hands of the Prussians in 1864, and Norway's failure to offer any assistance to the Danes in their hour of need, filled Ibsen with a deep sense of outrage (compounded perhaps by feelings of guilt at his own personal failure to offer any tangible assistance to his fellow Scandinavians). This smouldering outrage, contrasting with the relative peace and calm of Rome, proved to be a fertile seed bed for his two dramatic poems exploring the nature of human will-power, commitment and freedom.

In his later life, Ibsen claimed to his English translator William Archer and to his biographer Hans Jæger that the most important model for Brand was the dissenting priest Lammers who had founded a break-away movement from the established church in Skien during the 1840s. He denied vigorously that Brand was modelled on the life of

40

the Danish philosopher Søren Kierkegaard. Despite his protestations, however, there are many obvious parallels in both *Brand* and *Peer Gynt* with Kierkegaard's main philosophical preoccupations.

Regarded by some today as the first existentialist philosopher, Kierkegaard had stressed the primacy of human will-power and freedom to choose, even in the face of absurdity and naked terror. He had underlined the importance of man's subjectivity and the need for each individual to choose his mode of being-in-the-world with passionate commitment. In *Either-Or* (*Enten-eller*, 1843) and *Stages on Life's Way* (*Stadier paa Livets Vej*, 1845) he had identified three primary modes of response: the aesthetic, the ethical and the religious. He had also illustrated what these modes of response meant in terms of actual experience. In making his demand that man should choose his way of life with passionate intensity, Kierkegaard was less interested in whether one mode of response was intrinsically better than another (even if he clearly stated that it was). What mattered was the quality of each individual's commitment to his chosen way of life. The lack of passionate commitment in contemporary religious (and political) institutions appalled Kierkegaard. What he demanded of those who had chosen the path of religion was the ability to face up to the absolute paradox of faith in an absurd universe. As he expressed it in *Fear and Trembling*: 'to make the movements of faith [I must] shut my eyes and plunge confidently into the absurd'.

This leap of faith could not be taken once and for all, but needed constant reaffirmation. It brought no certainty, only anguish, as man was required to make his choices in the face of conflicting evidence. In extreme cases, this might even involve what Kierkegaard called in *Fear and Trembling*, 'a teleological suspension of the ethical', where

41

man was required by his faith in God to commit what might seem to be an unethical deed. The example he cites is that of Abraham required by God to offer up his beloved son Isaac as a sacrifice to God's will. Is this a sinful temptation, or his solemn duty?

As John Macquarrie has pointed out, the conflict Abraham experiences is essentially a conflict between two levels of conscience: conscience, on the one hand, as his awareness of the accepted moral code of his society, and conscience, on the other, as his belief in a deeper imperative in which God's will and his own self-awareness are linked.[1] In order to obey this deeper imperative, he must risk transgressing the normally accepted ethics of human conduct. But it is only in facing up to the terror in such paradoxes that men discover the true inwardness of faith, arriving at a harmony that transcends reason. As Kierkegaard sees it, when man plunges resolutely into the abyss, he finds that he has plunged into the 'open arms of God'.

In both *Brand* and *Peer Gynt* Ibsen reflects many of the insights built into the fabric of Kierkegaard's work: notably his critique of modern secular and religious authority and his contempt for those who seem incapable of making conscious, whole-hearted choices. Brand castigates such people in his speeches, while the whole play *Peer Gynt* revolves around that theme. *Brand* also explores at some length the differences between an aesthetic and an ethical response to life, much as Kierkegaard had outlined them in *Either-Or.* However, in putting forward his arguments, Kierkegaard ultimately places greater stress on 'essence' rather than 'existence', which makes him more of an idealist than an existentialist. It is here that Ibsen takes issue with Kierkegaard.

Whatever terrors confront man in Kierkegaard's world

picture, whatever anguish is produced by the burden of choice facing him, in the last analysis God is there to sustain him. There *is* an angel with the ram in the gorse bush, which means that Abraham is spared the agony of having to sacrifice Isaac. For Ibsen, there is no angel and no ram. When Brand is confronted by a similar dilemma to Abraham, his 'teleological suspension of the ethical' leads directly to the death of his own son. In Ibsen's world picture, there is no divine essence to safeguard man in his hour of need; man has to define himself and his values by his deeds.

'Brand'

Brand is more an exploration of a theme than a detailed study of characters or relationships. It has an abstract, highly patterned feel to it. The rhyming verse is tightly controlled, with at times an epigrammatic quality that imprints certain key notions and concepts indelibly on one's consciousness. (Some of this effect is lost in translation. Compare, for instance, the rhythmic insistence, the rhymed precision and expressive terseness of Brand's last lines in Act 4: 'Tabets alt din vinding skabte; – / evigt ejes kun det tabte!' with the best of the modern English translations: 'The loss of All brought everything to you . . ./ Only what is lost can be possessed for ever!' [iii, p. 194]. The sense is adequately conveyed, but not the chiselled economy and the dramatic pulse of the language.) In production, the verse stands out in sharp relief against the stylised background of a mountain and fjord landscape. In *Brand*, the language is the action.

Thematically, the play revolves around the juxtaposition of love and will-power. Brand consistently asserts the primacy of will-power and commitment in human affairs.

The action of the play, however, demonstrates that the only way to God is through love, not will-power: love of life, love of one's fellows, love of one's nearest and dearest. Act 1, played out amongst the crags and snow-covered precipices of a mountain landscape, sets up a morality play struggle between Brand and three types of evil: faint-heartedness, frivolity and wildness. Each of these qualities is embodied in a specific character: the peasant, the artist, and the gypsy girl Gerd. In Acts 2 to 4, set in an isolated fjord village, Brand is shown testing his will-power in the face of environmental and family determinism. We see him standing head and shoulders above the weak-willed men of compromise in the village community, but we also see his harshness towards his mother and his wife Agnes. There is no compassion in his dealings with others. Act 5 shows Brand finally rejecting all the compromises of contemporary society, as he leads his flock of parishioners into the mountain peaks. All too soon, they turn against him and reject him. Deserted in this mythical landscape, Brand faces the voice of his own conscience and examines his past deeds and responses. In the closing moments of the play, he discovers that God is not a God of Wrath, but a God of Love.

At an early stage in the action, Ibsen raises a question about the authenticity of Brand's ethics. Brand insists on the primacy of will, but Ibsen suggests that this insistence may be a sign of weakness not of strength. He shows us how Brand's personality has been moulded by a heritage of guilt, conditioning his responses to others and even determining the nature of his beliefs and ideals. In Act 2, we learn how his mother sacrificed her whole life to a dream of wealth that proved to be completely illusory, marrying a man for a fortune he never possessed. Reared in this loveless home, with the childhood memory of his mother desperately searching for the supposed hidden treasure under the mattress of her dead husband, Brand has grown up with a dark and pessimistic vision of life. He cannot understand the warmth of grace and charity; as he sees it, religion can only be interpreted in the bleakest terms of sin and retribution. He is already a victim of his past when the play opens.

Brand's wife Agnes first teaches him how to love. Through her he learns that one must love another in order to love all others. In her daily life Agnes had the ability to see greatness in small things, to clasp together earth and heaven with a spontaneity he can never achieve. Only after her death, at the beginning of Act 5, does he realise the value of her innate grace and charity. Even then, however, he cannot convert his insight into action. Brand sees himself as an Abraham called upon absurdly to sacrifice all he loves to a jealous God. But where Abraham is spared from having to make his sacrifice, Brand offers up his son and his wife in a sacrifice that is both meaningless and pointless. Like Kierkegaard's hero in *Fear and Trembling*, Brand trusts his deepest instincts in his attempts to discover and execute God's will; but having made his leap of faith, he finds himself, not in the open arms of God, but trapped in a vortex of bitterness, misunderstanding and un-acknowledged grief.

After Agnes's death, Brand finds himself moving further away from humanity. In Act 5, the official church's exploitation of religion as a means of keeping people orderly and quiet provokes Brand into leading his parishioners into the mountains. But all he can offer them is a crown of thorns. Not surprisingly, they reject and stone him. Eventually it takes the mad gypsy girl Gerd to spell out to him the hubris of which he is guilty. He sees himself in his heart as a new Messiah come to redeem the world with his

45

suffering. In reality, he is a man whose inability to respond warmly and lovingly to others has driven him away from human society altogether. His last refuge is an ice church, his only companion a deranged gypsy girl who unleashes an avalanche on them both by firing her rifle.

As a figure, Brand has towered far above the petty and mean-spirited individuals in his community. And yet he is as much a part of erring humanity as any of the lesser figures, such as the Mayor or the Dean, who appear in caricature beside him. He too, like the rest of humanity, is burdened with a heritage of guilt that can distort even the noblest ideals:

> To be myself entirely? But what about that burden,
> The weight of one's inheritance of guilt?   [iii, p. 115]

The question was to preoccupy Ibsen for the rest of his creative life. Repeatedly he was to return to the theme of idealism and vocation, corroded by a personal heritage of guilt. But invariably he implies in his work that there is a path to insight and fulfilment through the medium of authentically shared human experience. Even though many of his characters refuse to open themselves to others and refuse to acknowledge the potential for change within themselves (preferring instead the safety of conventionally sanctioned patterns of thought and behaviour), the possibility is always there, and it is that possibility that provides the creative tension in his work.

Despite his admiration for Brand (and arguably Kierkegaard) as idealists, Ibsen suggests in his play that it is 'existence' and not 'essence' that matters. We define ourselves in the way we live, think and respond to others and not in obeying some deep intuition of God's will. The remarkable achievement of the play was to explore with great sympathy many of the key issues Kierkegaard had raised in his work, while at the same time expressing profound reservations about the central insight underpinning Kierkegaard's philosophy.

'Peer Gynt'

Peer Gynt is built closely around a Biblical text (and at the time Ibsen was preparing himself to write *Brand* and *Peer Gynt* he admitted in a letter to Bjørnson that he read nothing but the Bible). The text is from Matthew 16, v 25: 'For whosoever will save his life shall lose it'. Expressed in the words of the Buttonmoulder in Act 5 of *Peer Gynt*, this is paraphrased as: 'To be one's self is to slay one's self'. *Peer Gynt* is written as a subjective morality play, structured around this theme. Acts 1 to 3 concentrate on Peer's youth; Act 4 on his middle age; and Act 5 on his old age.

Although the exploration of an abstract theme is Ibsen's major concern in *Peer Gynt*, the figure of Peer is so lively and vivacious that the play can be read as an extended character study. What fascinates an audience or a reader is the breathtaking scale of Peer's mercurial evasions and acts of self-deception. As in *Brand*, the rhyming verse fully expresses the action, although in *Peer Gynt* the verse is no longer terse and epigrammatic but expansive and witty as Peer indulges in long flights of fancy and tumbles from one set of experiences and responses to another. The effect is of a glittering verbal cascade, as fanciful descriptive passages alternate with a series of amusing encounters between Peer and a series of real and imaginary characters.

In contrast to the visual austerity of *Brand*, the physical setting of *Peer Gynt* is both attractive and stimulating. The play offers a constantly changing kaleidoscope of contrasting visual images: the fertile Gudbrandsdal of central Norway, the imaginary kingdom of the trolls, a luxury yacht at anchor off the coast of North Africa, the Sahara desert, a madhouse in Cairo, a shipwreck off the coast of Norway. For actor and director, there is ample opportunity in *Peer Gynt* to underline or comment on the action in visual terms. *Brand*, with its gaunt, static setting, places greater stress on the hammer-like impact of the verse.

Peer lives out his life at a level of unthinking selfishness. He cannot envisage behaving in any other way than that of gratifying his every whim and caprice. He turns his life into a fairy tale and finds it quite impossible to distinguish between fantasy and reality. He is the archetypal representative of Kierkegaard's aesthetic man for whom the world and other people only matter in so far as they provide him with physical or emotional stimulation. He can only exploit others, he cannot relate to any one. His early progression in the first two acts of the play is therefore from drink and fantasy to bride rape and sexual orgy (with three sæter girls on the high mountains). He ends up appropriately in the latter part of Act 2 in the court of the Troll King, the arch representative in the play of ugly self-centredness. As far as Peer is concerned, the world is peopled by trolls, which is why he may as well become one. But only if it costs him nothing. When he discovers that the trolls intend scratching his eye to ensure that his vision is suitably distorted, he recoils in terror. Peer is not prepared to commit himself to anything, particularly if it means accepting responsibility for the way he lives.

As in *Brand*, Ibsen explains Peer's behaviour in terms of family determinism. Peer's father, Jon Gynt, was a drunken spendthrift who squandered the fortune he had inherited (there is almost certainly an oblique reference to Ibsen's own father here). While he was out carousing, his wife Åse took refuge from her responsibilities in fairy tales and fantasies, as she herself acknowledges in Act 2:

> The best we could do was try and forget it;
> I never was good at standing firm.
> It's frightful, looking life in the eye;
> Better to shrug worry off if you can,
> And try not to think too much about it.
> So either you take to the bottle, or lies;
> That's it: we made do with fairy stories
> About princes and trolls and birds and beasts;
> And bride-stealing, too. But who would have thought
> Those infernal tales would have clung to him so?
>
> [iii, p. 286]

Peer has acquired essentially his mother's response to life. And their early sharing of family misfortune has bound him to her in a way that is emotionally disabling. It is as if he cannot escape from her and the fantasy refuge she once created for them both. When in trouble, he always runs back to her or calls to her for help. In large measure, it is his dependence on his mother that makes it impossible for him to establish viable adult relationships with anyone else.

In Act 1, Peer meets a young girl called Solvejg who is chaste and pure. She becomes for him almost a mother substitute, which is why he dare not possess her physically even though she is willing to commit herself to him. His rutting thoughts intervene when he is alone with Solvejg. In his mind, he conjures up images of sordid sexual experiences from the troll world and he cannot cope with the conflicting emotions this produces.

After the death of his mother in Act 3, and with troll memories ruining any hope of a relationship with Solvejg, Peer once more flees into a life of selfish exploitation of others. We see the effects of this in Act 4 when he is shown as an amoral business tycoon, only too willing to betray people and principles to increase his personal profit.

In Act 5, Peer, who is now an old man, is confronted by a series of purgatorial experiences that force him to reassess his life and achievements. The strange passenger on the boat, the meeting with Solvejg as an old woman, the buttonmoulder who wants to melt him down because he has been such a failure in life – all these make him pause and think about who and what he is. For the first time in his life, he experiences adult fear and terror. At which point, Ibsen is once again back within the framework of Kierkegaard's philosophy.

In *The Concept of Dread*, Kierkegaard had explored at length how dread or *angst* was both a sign of man's awareness of his sinfulness and the necessary prelude to becoming aware of the need for grace. Coming face to face with Solvejg, Peer cries out: 'O truth! And time can't be redeemed! / O terror! Here's where my empire was!' [iii, p. 397]. Even the vocabulary is Kierkegaardian at this moment of recognition. What follows is a dialogue of the spirit as Peer wrestles with himself and the voices of his conscience. Has he truly fulfilled himself? Or has he simply squandered his potential? What is the real essence of Peer Gynt? In order to find his real self, Peer resolves at the end of the play to commit himself to Solvejg. It is the first conscious decision he has ever made and might therefore be interpreted as his progression from the aesthetic to the ethical mode of being.

To read the play in this manner, as many critics have done, would make it a flawless demonstration of Kierkegaard's ideas. But the ending is more problematic than this. In committing himself to Solvejg, Peer is still in large measure seeking protection from the reality of what he has done, and therefore what he has become, in a dream image of wife and mother: 'My mother; my wife; purest of women! / Hide me there, hide me in your heart!' [iii, p. 421]. If his Empire all the time was a dream image of wife and mother, then Peer even at the end of the play has arguably still not progressed beyond the nursery.

Once again, Ibsen appears to have made extensive and sympathetic use in this play of Kierkegaard's insight while querying the experiential basis of that insight. Even conscious choice can still amount to a flight from real experience when one chooses an abstract essence in preference to actual existence (in Peer's case, a dream image of wife and mother instead of a real wife of flesh and blood). Perhaps that is why the Buttonmoulder remains unconvinced at the end of the play by Peer's conversion: 'We shall meet at the last cross-road, Peer; / And *then* we'll see whether – ; I say no more' [iii, p. 421]. Here, and in *Brand*, Ibsen preferred to remain a philosophical sceptic, leaving his audiences and readers with a series of paradoxes that they themselves would have to resolve. As he was to state in his poem *A rhyming letter* (*Et rimbrev*, 1875), he preferred to ask, not to answer.

'Emperor and Galilean'

The one occasion on which he did attempt to provide an answer in his work was in *Emperor and Galilean*. He himself drew attention to the fact in a letter to his publisher in July 1871: 'This work will be my masterpiece, it is occupying all my thoughts and all my time. The positive "Weltanschauung" that the critics have long demanded of me will be found there'. *Emperor and Galilean* was a play that had occupied his mind for almost a decade. Stylistically, it marked the turning point in his work between

51

romanticism and realism. He deliberately abandoned the verse forms of *Brand* and *Peer Gynt* in favour of prose dialogue. As he explained to Edmund Gosse in 1874: 'What I wanted to portray was people and it was precisely for that reason that I did not allow them to speak with "the tongues of angels" ' [iv, p. 606]. Philosophically, however, the play relied heavily on the romantic idealism of Hegel.

Ibsen had first encountered Hegel's ideas as a student in Christiania where the professor of philosophy at the university, M. J. Monrad, was a committed follower of Hegel's. It is also highly likely that Ibsen had read Heiberg's essay on *Human Freedom* (1824), which was a Hegelian analysis of freedom and necessity. Ibsen admitted in a letter to Julius Hoffory in 1888 that *Emperor and Galilean* was written, 'under the influence of German cultural life'. The action of the play is underpinned by an unmistakably Hegelian sense of the individual's relationship to the world will.

In his *Phenomenology of Spirit* (*Phänomenologie des Geistes*, 1806) and *Philosophy of History* (*Philosophie der Geschichte*, 1832), Hegel outlined the notion of world history as a dialectical progression of the spirit, a dynamic clash of opposites in which the world will made itself manifest and achieved its overall purpose. As thesis provoked antithesis, the clash was resolved in a synthesis that would in time become a new thesis. Underneath the apparent disunity was the all-embracing unity of the spirit, working through the clash of opposing forces. Individuals, acting in complete freedom, were instruments of the Spirit, the world will, as they ushered in new ideas that contributed to the onward thrust of spiritual progress.

In Hegel's tragic theory, tragedy ensues from the clash between the powers that have absolute and ideal authority in man's spiritual world: 'the eternal religious and ethical modes of relationship, status, personal character, and in the world of romance, before everything else, honour and love'.[2] These ideal substances or values have become clothed in human flesh, embodied in individual characters, and it is the clash between ideal values (e.g. the demands of state, family, love and honour) that should form the basis of tragedy. Not then a clash between good and evil, but between good and good. The Absolute invariably asserts its essential unity at the end of a tragedy by achieving a sense of reconciliation, even at the expense of individual suffering. What is rejected is not the ideals with which the tragic hero may have identified himself, but rather the one-sided and imbalanced assertion of the ideal.

Another possible source of Hegelian ideas can be found in the plays and theory of Hebbel, a dramatist who had been strongly recommended to Ibsen as a model by Hermann Hettner. Hebbel's ideas on tragedy, while derived from Hegel's work, nevertheless differed importantly from those of Hegel. In his short essay *A Word on Drama* (*Ein Wort über das Drama*, 1843), Hebbel asserted that the real business of tragedy was to explore the relationship between the individual will and the world will, showing how any assertion of individual will invariably provokes a counterbalancing assertion of the world will. Dramatic guilt was therefore the result of the individual asserting his own will and had nothing to do with sin or unethical behaviour: 'it derives directly from the will itself, from any act of obstinate, arbitrary self-assertion'. In the concluding paragraph of his essay, Hebbel explained that his overall aim was to write a type of drama that would combine the social, historical and philosophical, without giving undue emphasis to any one sphere of interest.

It is not difficult to see how the ideas of both Hegel and Hebbel have found their way into the fabric of *Emperor and Galilean*. Written in two parts, the play is set at a turning point in history, when Julian the Apostate attempted to halt the onward thrust of Christianity by reintroducing pagan culture and religion into Eastern Roman civilisation. In Part I, Acts 1 to 2 Julian is shown as a young prince who feels disillusioned in the oppressive atmosphere of Constantinople. For him, the new truth of Christianity is no longer true, while in Athens he discovers that the old beauties of Dionysus worship are no longer beautiful.

In Act 3, the mystic Maximus outlines a dialectical mission for him in a visionary séance. He is to found a new empire, a third empire: 'which shall be founded on the tree of knowledge and the tree of the cross together, because it hates and loves them both, and because it has its living springs under Adam's grove and Golgotha' [iv, p. 259]. He is to found this empire by freely willing what must be, freely submitting himself to the law of necessity.

But there are conflicting signs and portents. Julian has already experienced a spectacular vision in which he sees himself as a spiritual ruler completing the task of Moses, Alexander and Christ. Maximus, on the other hand, sees a vision of three figures whom he calls, 'corner stones under the wrath of necessity'. Cain and Judas Iscariot are the first two: the third is still alive. The first two had to will freely what they did because of what they were. They were the agents of necessity. The clear implication is that Julian could well be the third, 'great helper in denial'. Despite this conflict of signs (expressed in the Norwegian as 'tegn imod tegn' – 'sign against sign'), Julian chooses to believe only the positive signs and, at the end of Part I, commits himself to make a bid for power in the name of Helios the Sun God. The result, traced out in Part 2 of the play, is a spiral towards disaster.

On becoming Emperor, Julian chooses to embrace pagan beliefs and rituals as a first step towards reconciling the conflicting demands of Dionysus and Christ. But the resolute opposition of the Christians leaves little scope for reconciliation. Julian is driven to use force against the Christians and to impose pagan worship on them. This leads to armed conflict, culminating in a large battle where Julian is killed. After his death, Maximus sums up the central insight of the play:

> Led astray like Cain. Led astray like Judas. . . . Your God is a wasteful god, Galileans! He is lavish with souls. Were you, Julian, not the right one, this time either . . . sacrificed on the altar of necessity? [. . .] To *will* is to *have to will*. [iv, p. 458]

Quite clearly, one can see Julian as a tragic hero in the manner of Hebbel. His obstinate acts of self-assertion are not in themselves ethically wrong or sinful. But they provoke a series of massive counterbalancing assertions of the world will. He becomes a victim of necessity in a drama that links, as Hebbel desired, the social, historical and philosophical.

More subtly one can detect the influence of Hegel's dramatic theories. Julian feels within him the conflicting pull of juxtaposed absolutes – the beauty of Dionysus worship, the truth of Christ's teachings. His attempt to reconcile the two leads him to choose one rather than the other as a dominant mode of being. But the undue emphasis he places on pagan beauty (albeit because of Christian opposition) leads to social and political imbalance. Neither value is intrinsically wrong or evil and neither is completely rejected in the play. What is rejected is Julian's extreme advocacy of one set of values. After his death, he is seen, not as an evil man brought low, but as 'a glorious shattered instrument of the Lord'. His death restores a sense of balance to a society that had become increasingly fragmented and chaotic, bringing with it peace and reconciliation. Even Maximus, who most passionately mourns his passing, feels some sense of tragic reconciliation: 'The third empire shall come! The spirit of man shall reclaim its heritage . . . and burnt offerings shall be made for you and your two guests in the symposium' [iv, p. 458].

Unlike *Brand* and *Peer Gynt*, there seems to be in *Emperor and Galilean* no ironic or critical distance from the philosophical ideas informing the work. The play is a closely argued embodiment of Hegel's dialectical method. That is in itself a remarkable achievement, which helps to explain why Ibsen felt so proud of it. But complex philosophical ideas, given dramatic shape and expression, do not necessarily form an ideal basis for aesthetically satisfying works of art. There are moments of considerable dramatic power in the play, notably in the final acts of both parts; there are also scenes in both parts that offer ample scope for imaginative visual comment on stage. However, by comparison with Ibsen's two great poetic dramas, *Emperor and Galilean* seems generally flat and laboured; it is very much a flawed masterpiece.

The importance of the play for Ibsen lay in the ideas it embodied, and he returned to these in his late work. In *Hedda Gabler*, for instance, Hedda pursues a pagan ideal of beauty with a destructive lack of balance that is reminiscent of Julian's behaviour. She even takes over his image of Dionysian youths dancing with vine leaves in their hair. In *The Master Builder*, Solness, like Julian, is a man faced with a number of crucial choices; but in his life too the signs and portents conflict. In his confusion, Solness chooses to assert himself in a way that invites dire retribution from the world will.

In 1872, while Ibsen was completing his work on *Emperor and Galilean*, he was sent a book that was profoundly to influence his attitude to playwriting and the whole future direction of his work: Georg Brandes's *Main Currents of Nineteenth-century Literature*, a monumental work in which Denmark's leading literary critic outlined an unorthodox and challenging view of modern literary history, with the declared aim of helping a progressive and radical spirit to 'break through' in Scandinavian writing. (The term 'break through', or 'Gennembrud' in Danish, became Brandes's slogan for progressive writing.) The radicalism of Brandes's ideas infuriated the conservative establishment in Copenhagen, but proved a fertile source of inspiration to Ibsen. He described *Main Currents*, in a letter to Brandes in April 1872, as: 'one of the books that sets a yawning chasm between yesterday and today'.

In his inaugural lecture, printed in Denmark as the introduction to *Main Currents*, Brandes outlined his aim as follows: 'The principal task will be to direct into our country, through a multiplicity of channels, those currents originating in the revolution and in the belief in progress and to halt the reaction at every point where, historically, its mission is at an end'. His charge was that Scandinavian literature was imprisoned in outmoded patterns of thought and expression, derived mainly from Romanticism. Such was the power of outdated Romantic attitudes that even a potentially revolutionary nature like Ibsen had been misled, in *Brand*, into exploring a romantic idealistic quest. Progressive thinkers in France above all were directing their spiritual energies to the present and to the complex problems confronting modern man: problems involving marriage and property, problems relating to a whole range of social and sexual relationships. Axiomatically, Brandes asserted that modern literature only has life and vitality when it 'submits problems to debate'.

Ibsen was already wrestling with the task of finding a dramatic form that would more adequately give expression to the interrelated spheres of the social, the historical and the philosophical (hence his decision in *Emperor and Galilean* to use prose rather than verse). Brandes's inaugural lecture therefore served to clarify ideas that were already preoccupying him, giving him a clear-cut programme for his future work. For the next two decades he was to explore in his plays a variety of modern social and marital problems in a way that entirely fulfilled the demands Brandes had made for a progressive, social-realist approach to writing.

On the other hand, Ibsen never entirely forsook his romantic past. Through Brandes, he became aware of modern French determinist thinking, embodied above all in the works of Hippolyte Taine and Emile Zola. Some of his social plays (notably *A Doll's House* and *Ghosts*) reflect aspects of determinist thought, with characters seen in large measure as the product of their environment or physical inheritance. Even so, Ibsen never relinquished his belief in the power of individual choice and commitment. While Taine in his *History of English Literature* (1863) might see man exclusively as the product of three great determining forces – *la race*, *le milieu* and *le moment* – Ibsen saw man, even in his ostensibly naturalist plays, as an ultimately free agent, capable of changing his patterns of thought and response, despite the pressure of environment or circumstances. Brandes himself acknowledged as much in an essay he wrote on Ibsen's work in 1882:

When he touches a social sore, as in *The Pillars of*

Society, and elsewhere, it is always one of a moral nature. Some one is to blame for it. [. . .] Hence Ibsen, looking on the world as bad, feels no compassion for men, only indignation. His pessimism is not of a metaphysical, but of a moral nature, and is based on a conviction of the possibility of realising ideals; it is, in a word, the pessimism of indignation. And his want of sympathy with many kinds of suffering results from his conviction of the educative power of suffering. Only through suffering can these small, miserable men become great.[3]

This tension between man's moral freedom, on the one hand, and the determining effects of environment or personal heritage, on the other, was to provide the essential intellectual framework for Ibsen's mature plays. It was the ground bass against which he wove his imaginatively resonant variations in each successive play. A similar tension had already informed his writing of *Brand*, *Peer Gynt* and *Emperor and Galilean*, even though these were written under the impact of widely differing philosophical systems. Despite the different philosophical influences on Ibsen, and despite his changing understanding of the nature of determinism, what did not change was his commitment to the notion of human agency, freedom and responsibility. With some justice he could and did claim that his work should be read as a cohesive whole.

4
Dolls' Houses

In a speech he made to the Norwegian Women's Rights League in May 1898, Ibsen claimed that he had been 'more of a poet and less of a social philosopher' than people generally seemed inclined to believe. Such was the effectiveness with which he had submitted problems to debate in his plays during the late 1870s and the 1880s that people tended to forget that he was above all a poet of the theatre, a master craftsman who exploited in his work all the expressive possibilities of the theatre – movement, placing, setting, light and colour – to express his insight into human lives and destinies.

However, it was as a social dramatist that Ibsen first made a substantial impact on the literary consciousness of contemporary Europe, with *Pillars of Society* in 1877, *A Doll's House* in 1879 and *Ghosts* in 1881. These were the plays that established his reputation as Europe's leading and most controversial playwright. Following Brandes's advice in his inaugural lecture, Ibsen concentrated his attention in these three plays on modern social and marital problems, showing the close inter-relationship between public and private morality. His main focus of attention was contemporary middle-class society, and he exposed its hidden assumptions, its inadequacies and its destructive pressures with the precision of a skilled surgeon.

In his social plays, Ibsen was particularly concerned with the role of women in contemporary society. Although he never associated himself with the Norwegian feminists, he nevertheless wrote movingly and perceptively of the ways in which women were disadvantaged and exploited in contemporary society. In a speech he made at Trondheim in June 1885, he stated: 'The transformation of social conditions which is now being undertaken in the rest of Europe is very largely concerned with the future status of workers and of women' [vi, p. 447]. As an artist, he had little direct experience of working-class life, and it is therefore hardly surprising that working-class characters do not figure very largely in his plays. But as the son of a once wealthy merchant, he was able to observe at first hand the problems confronting middle-class women in the ruthlessly competitive world of nineteenth-century society.

'Pillars of Society'

In the first of his great social plays, *Pillars of Society*, he took the for him unusual step of exploring in parallel the problems facing both women and the working classes in the nascent capitalist society of Norway in the late 1870s. Capitalism had come late to Norway, but its rapid development during the latter half of the nineteenth century transformed an economically backward country, dependent on agriculture, fishing, forestry and shipping, into an economically successful but socially divided industrial nation. The transformation was in large measure

61

effected by a small group of powerful men (mostly of foreign merchant stock) who acquired industrial and trading empires spanning many different areas.[1] Ibsen takes one such magnate as his central character in the play, Consul Bernick, and shows the effects of his policies on a typical small-town community in contemporary Norway.

His observation is meticulous and detailed, even down to the fact that Bernick is 'of foreign stock'. His grasp of key social issues is equally precise. At the very inception of industrial capitalism in Norway, Ibsen pinpoints the threat of redundancy through technological advance as the major worry of the newly created working class, represented in the play in the figure of Aune, the shipyard foreman. Ibsen also shows how the thrusting, though belated, development of capitalism in Norway was intimately linked with the puritan revival that swept the country in the mid-nineteenth century.[2] He demonstrates how the puritan ethic teaches both women, as guardians of the family, and paid workers, as the source of all surplus value, to be docile, inward-looking and suspicious of personal happiness and fulfilment. Meanwhile, we see the captains of industry cloaking their rapaciousness with a hypocritical veneer of moral respectability.

The new pietism that Ibsen saw as the handmaiden of industrial capitalism casts an oppressive gloom over Act 1. In a visual tableau as the play opens, we are shown a group of women imprisoned by their need to be seen doing good works. While they sew clothes for the fallen women of the town, they sit listening to an improving tale read out by Rørlund, a teacher who is the local apostle of puritan doctrine. All of them are frightened of betraying their real feelings and are almost ashamed to remember the golden days of their youth when there was merriment and light-hearted socialising in their little community.

The static and somewhat cowed role of the women in Act 1 is contrasted verbally and visually with the behaviour of their husbands. Initially, Bernick and his wealthy allies in town are heard arguing in an off-stage room while the women sit quietly sewing. When eventually the men burst into the room, it is to announce their latest strategy for industrial and economic development. They have decided to build a branch railway line to the town. We learn in the dialogue that Bernick had earlier exploited the pietist prejudices of the community to mobilise opinion against a coastal railway line to the town. This would have damaged his own shipping interests. Now, however, he has found a way of building an inland branch line that will avoid any damage to his coastal shipping line, while enabling him to reap the enormous benefits of further industrial development in the shape of mining and forestry.

Naturally, the women who are the appointed guardians of morality in the play are surprised at this volte-face. But Bernick silences any protests firmly, almost brusquely: 'My dear Betty, it's not a thing for the ladies to worry their heads about'. His vision of family life is entirely patriarchal. It is his duty to build an industrial empire and his wife's duty to be supportive both domestically and socially. While he and his partners engage in speculative ventures of dubious validity, the role of their wives is to project an image of kindly respectability by dispensing charity to the fallen and destitute. Awkward questions are decidedly unwelcome.

Throughout the whole of Act 1, Ibsen reinforces in visual terms the contrasting role of Bernick and the women. While the latter sit in static groups, moving from the sewing table to the coffee table in the garden, Bernick strides across the stage like a feudal lord through his domain, mingling business and pleasure in swift succession. His use of the stage space is purposeful and calculated, and he is adept at arranging suitable tableaux of domestic harmony to project into the outside world through his plate-glass windows.

The ordered stability of Bernick's world is threatened at the end of Act 1 by the unexpected arrival in town of his brother-in-law, Johan Tønnesen, and Lona Hessel, whom Bernick once loved and who knows too much about his past. Lona has returned from America with Johan. Her casual dress and the decisive manner in which she opens the curtains, windows and doors in Bernick's drawing room, 'to let in some fresh air', signal a visual challenge to all that Bernick and his community represent. A substantial part of the action in the remainder of the play revolves around Lona's attempts to make Bernick face up to the reality of what he has done and hence what he has become: a man living a private and public lie.

In Act 2, Bernick admits to Lona that he once abandoned her in favour of her wealthy half-sister Betty because he needed Betty's money for the family firm. He also admits that he had an affair with an actress and allowed Johan to take the blame. After Johan's departure for America, he agrees that he may have helped to spread the rumour that Johan had embezzled money from the family firm. That rumour and Betty's money helped the firm to survive. On the basis of these private lies, Bernick has prospered and built up an economic empire. Since then he has acted on the basis of a public lie, namely that he has been motivated in his business deals by the aim of benefiting the community.

Confronted by Lona's challenge to his authority, Bernick fiercely resists any change. He makes no concessions in his arguments with her. He is even willing to contemplate murder to silence Johan and safeguard his own reputation (allowing him to sail to America on *The Indian Girl*, a patched-up hulk that will never reach its destination). And yet, despite such decisive actions, he refuses to accept any responsibility for what he does. He sees himself as nothing more than a tool in the hands of the community, his deeds and thoughts entirely determined by social pressures: 'Isn't it society itself that forces us into these devious ways?' [v, p. 89].

The link between Bernick's private and public life is firmly established in Act 2. Ibsen draws a clear parallel between Bernick's attitude to his wife and to his shipyard workers. In both cases he is arrogant and patronising, manipulating and exploiting his wife and his employees to his own advantage. In both cases he also claims that he is acting for the good of the community.

It takes the threat of a personal tragedy to jolt him out of this pattern. His son Olaf stows away on *The Indian Girl*. And although the ship is stopped in time, the thought that he might have murdered his own child in attempting to save his reputation brings him to reassess his behaviour and his motives. In Act 4 we are shown the results of this reassessment.

As the citizens gather, in a carefully stage-managed torchlight procession, to pay homage to him as a pillar of the community, Bernick makes a public confession of his past and present misdeeds. He admits to the craving for power behind his activities and confesses his self-interest in the various land deals associated with the new railway line. On the other hand, he astutely claims that he still feels best qualified to administer the development of the new line. Finally, he confesses his earlier sin in seducing an actress belonging to a visiting troupe of players.

This fourth-act repentance has led most critics to view *Pillars of Society* as a thesis play written in the manner of Augier or Dumas *fils*. Certainly the structure and the plot with its numerous reversals and surprises follows the complicated pattern they perfected. But there is a strong ironic current running through the whole play, an almost mischievous sense of parody that contrasts effectively with scenes of emotional intensity (the mingling of laughter and tears is at times reminiscent of Chekhov). Bernick may indeed have accepted responsibility for his past deeds in his speech, but his confession is astutely worded and leaves him in remarkably good shape.

What he has achieved by the end of the play is to be left in sole control of the new railway line, having effectively excluded his former partners. He binds his family even closer to him than before. And he also manages to persuade Lona Hessel, the one woman he ever loved, to stay on in a questionable *ménage à trois*. Meanwhile, Aune the ship-yard foreman meekly accepts the use of new machines. The one thing Bernick does not confess in public is that he was prepared to stoop to murder in order to safeguard his position. That is a secret he shares with the cowed Aune.

At the end of the play, Bernick can rest assured that there will be no further industrial unrest in his shipyards, having overawed his workers by the breathless dexterity of his manoeuvres. He also has the satisfaction of knowing that the patriarchal family has been strengthened. Surrounded by happy and admiring women, he finds yet another rhetorical phrase to keep real experience at a distance: 'As for us . . . we have a long and hard day's work ahead of us. Particularly me. But let it come. Just as long as my two loyal and true-hearted women stand by me. That's something else I've learnt these last few days; it's you women who are the pillars of society' [v, p. 126].

The hopes for a new start that Bernick has expressed must have a large question mark beside them. Has he genuinely accepted responsibility for his actions, or is he still living in a protective fantasy where the support or the pressure of others determines how he will act? The ending of the play is highly ambiguous, although it is only in recent years that critics have become aware of its ironic undertones.[3]

After *Pillars of Society*, Ibsen never again divided his attention as a dramatist between the problems confronting women and the working classes in contemporary Norway. From then on he concentrated his attention on the role and status of women as a gauge of social development.

In *Pillars of Society* he had drawn a sympathetic portrait of a young woman who refused to be imprisoned in a conventional marriage. Dina Dorf, fleeing to America with Johan Tønnesen, spells out the conditions on which she will agree to marry him: 'Yes, I will be your wife. [. . .] But first I want to work . . . and make something of my life, as you have done. I don't just want to be a thing, there for the taking' [v, p. 107]. Clearly, for Ibsen this represented a vision of an ideal marriage, based on mutual respect, freedom and responsibility – the values he had always prized. In his later plays, all too few women are able to achieve anything even vaguely approximating to this ideal state. The few who do are for the most part women who have already experienced one disastrous marriage or relationship and have learnt, by bitter experience, to be self-reliant. For the majority of women in Victorian Europe, the outlook, as Ibsen described it in his plays, was bleak. In a series of tightly structured, carefully chiselled works of art, he showed his frequently shocked audiences images of women who were the victims of bourgeois conventions and attitudes, imprisoned in a series of doll's house marriages.

His next play was appropriately called *A Doll's House*, but it was only the first of a series exploring the built-in tensions of modern family life. The relationships explored in these different plays have a number of features in common. The families involved live isolated from the world around them because of their desire for the 'privilege' of privacy. Marriages are entered into for reasons of property or status. Once married, the women find they have a clearly defined and essentially subordinate role in relation to their men, whose property they legally and socially become. The common assumption of the men is that women are incapable of thinking logically and analytically (an assumption Ibsen seems to share in his notes for *A Doll's House*); on the other hand, the men lack the intuitive insight of their women and therefore tend to show an almost total disregard, with few exceptions, for the emotional needs and expectations of their partners.

Normally, it takes very little, by way of an emotional or social crisis, to disturb the fragile harmony of such marriages. It tends to be an everyday domestic crisis that sparks off a process of critical self-analysis in the various women who have hitherto unthinkingly accepted their inferior roles in marriage. Equally, in all of his problem plays, Ibsen uses the technical device of an outsider or friend or relative arriving in order to bring the crisis to a head.

'A Doll's House'

In *A Doll's House*, the arrival of Mrs Linde precipitates the crisis in the household of Torvald and Nora Helmer. Torvald Helmer is a successful young lawyer who has just been appointed the manager of a commercial bank. Commercial banks had only recently been developed in Norway;[4] the position of a bank manager was therefore a prestigious one at a time of rapid industrial and economic expansion. Torvald is understandably proud of his appointment but gives the impression of being somewhat pompous, self-centred and arrogant. He has been married for eight years, has three children and a pretty young wife called Nora.

The initial image we are given of Nora is of a doll wife, who plays skylarks and squirrels with her husband and revels in the thought of the various consumer luxuries she can at last permit herself now that Torvald has been promoted. She counteracts her husband's pompousness with kittenish flirtation and child-like acts of disobedience.

The action of the play follows a linear pattern until half-way through the third and final act. At that point, the various devices of the traditional well-made play are abandoned (the threatening presence of a moneylender, a fateful letter waiting in the letter box, a doctor friend in love with Nora and Nora's attempt to keep past secrets from her husband), and Nora and her husband sit down to talk through their marital problems for the first time in their eight years of marriage. The result is Nora's departure from the family home and the break-up of the marriage.

At various points in the action, characters are used to underline ironic parallels with the problems facing Nora and Torvald. Nora's friend Mrs Linde is a widow whose first marriage, contracted for purely financial reasons, was a disaster. Having learnt from that experience, she is prepared to commit herself freely and honestly to a man she has always loved even though he is spurned by society, namely the moneylender Krogstad. He is a widower. Despite hints that Krogstad may have a criminal past, Mrs Linde is prepared to share her life with him and his children. She feels they can meet each other's needs openly and frankly and in that way bring out the best in each other. The contrast with Nora's marriage is quite striking. Nora can only relate to her husband at the level of an irresponsible child. She can wheedle and cajole but can never speak to him frankly and has therefore had to take a number of serious decisions in her past life in secret and entirely on her own.

Dr Rank, a family friend, brings another parallel. He is a cynical pessimist, facing imminent death from an inherited disease. His fate reflects Nora's. He has inherited a disintegrating spine from his presumably syphilitic father. Nora, for her part, has acquired her 'irresponsible' attitudes and responses from her father's treatment of her. Rank's impending death is used to highlight the fact that Nora is thinking of committing suicide rather than bring 'disgrace' upon her husband. But where Rank learns nothing from his suffering and the certainty of his death – his attitude to people remains embittered and dismissive – Nora grows in stature from the experience of staring death in the face.

The play is full of visual suggestions that provide a comment on the action or underline a particular facet of a given character's responses.[5] We see something of Nora's extravagance in the Christmas presents she has bought and her excessive tipping of a porter. But in always buying the cheapest clothes we see her resourcefulness in making do. In eating forbidden macaroons she shows her defiance of Torvald, while in asking his advice about her costume for a fancy dress party, we see her skill in flattering and cajoling him. In showing her new silk stockings to Dr Rank, we see her willingness to flirt and exploit her sexuality, but not to the point where it becomes explicit. In her performance of the tarantella, we have an image of the dance of death, an image of the black thoughts filling her mind. The image is reinforced when she pulls a black shawl over her head before attempting to leave the house to commit suicide. Finally, her change of clothes and the donning of everyday dress underlines her determination in the last act of the play to face up to the prosaic reality of her marriage for the very first time.

At the heart of the play is a detailed exploration of Nora's character and the nature of her relationship with her husband. Underneath Nora's playful exterior, there is from the start an intuitively serious mind. Nora is totally committed to her children and to her husband. She knows his weaknesses and fully understands his need to feel in control. She therefore always humours him and helps him to feel that he takes all the important decisions in their life. In order to achieve this, she consciously plays out the role of a helpless scatterbrain. She is, however, quite capable of taking decisive action. When Torvald was desperately ill and needed a long convalescent journey to the South, he stubbornly refused to borrow money. Nora's usual cajoling tricks failed to make him change his mind. She therefore took action on her own account, borrowing the necessary money behind his back with the help of a forged signature. She did not stop to consider the ethical implications of her forgery: all that mattered to her was the health of her husband. Torvald was told that the money was a present from her father.

For Nora to sustain her submissive role vis-à-vis her husband, she needs to believe in him and in qualities that he would reveal in a crisis. In her imagination he becomes something of a courtly hero, albeit in domestic garb. Unfortunately, her commitment is based on romantic fantasy rather than reality. Deep down she suspects this herself, even though she would never consciously admit it. When a real crisis looms, namely Krogstad's threat to blackmail Torvald because of Nora's forgery, she prefers to contemplate suicide rather than put her husband's character to the test.

When the crisis breaks, her worst fears are confirmed. Torvald proves to be not a courtly hero, but a frightened and mean-spirited little man who is more worried about his reputation than his wife:

> Now you have ruined my entire happiness, jeopardized my whole future. It's terrible to think of. Here I am, at the mercy of a thoroughly unscrupulous person; he can do whatever he likes with me, demand anything he wants, order me about just as he chooses ... and I daren't even whimper. I'm done for, a miserable failure, and it's all the fault of a feather-brained woman!
>
> [v, p. 276]

In the confrontation that follows between husband and wife at the end of Act 3, Nora is in a state of shocked awareness. For the first time, she sees her life for what it is, and rejects it. She is determined to discover her real potential as a person, which means she has to reject the role of doll wife and doll mother. At the end of the play, she walks out on her husband and her children, leaving behind her a bewildered and confused man who is still completely imprisoned within the conditioned assumptions of his middle-class world. Torvald, we now see, is as much a victim as Nora, but he has not even begun to understand his predicament. The play closes with a question mark left in the audience's mind. Will Torvald ever learn to see and to understand in the way that his wife has, or will he continue to allow his responses and actions to be controlled by social conditioning?

Once again, Ibsen's major thematic concern was to explore the notion of freedom and responsibility juxtaposed with the inhibiting force of determinism. He does not underestimate the power of determinism, and there are two major characters in the play, Torvald and Dr Rank, who remain either bewildered or embittered victims of, in the one case, social, in the other, biological determinism. But the action of the play as a whole demonstrates the essential freedom of men and women to act decisively in shaping the quality of their lives and responses.

Despite the pressures of social and economic determinism, both Mrs Linde and Nora, in their diametrically opposed ways, make conscious and responsible choices about their future lives as a result of painfully acquired experience. In both cases, their future lives will be fraught with problems (Mrs Linde as a step-mother, married to a social outcast, and Nora, fending for herself as a shunned divorcee), but both women have demonstrated their ability to face up to difficulties and seek for authentic solutions.

A Doll's House was quite correctly interpreted by Ibsen's contemporaries as a swingeing attack on conventional bourgeois marriage (although importantly not on marriage *per se*). It was intended to be a profoundly revolutionary play, deepening the critique of patriarchal attitudes he had initiated in *Pillars of Society*. As Ibsen saw it, women would spearhead the revolt against the repressive conventions of contemporary society. Men were far more likely to be dominated by the social prejudices of their day because of their role as bread-winner and provider. That is why Nora consciously *acts* the part of a doll wife, whereas Torvald unthinkingly *lives out* his role as the authoritarian husband. By the same token, that also explains why Nora achieves insight at the end of the play, while her husband remains bewildered and confused.

Despite the conscious provocation within it, the play closes on an optimistic note. Nora has left with the positive aim of discovering who and what she is and what she can become. Meanwhile, there is at least a slender ray of hope that Torvald may yet achieve some degree of insight once he has recovered from the initial shock of his wife's departure. The question he articulates at the end sums up that hope and the difficulty implicit within it: 'The miracle of miracles . . .?' [v, p. 286].

It soon became clear to Ibsen, from the superficial nature of contemporary responses to *A Doll's House*, that people had not fully understood what was at stake behind the mildly optimistic, or at least open, ending of the play. The alternative, happy ending he was obliged to write for the German theatre was symptomatic of that. (He called this alternative ending, where Nora melts at the sight of her children, 'a barbaric outrage against the play'.)[6]

'Ghosts'

In his next play, *Ghosts*, he resolved to spell out in unmistakable terms what would happen to a woman like Nora who returned to her doll's house after an unsuccessful attempt at breaking free. As he commented in a letter to Sophie Adlersparre in June 1882: '*Ghosts had* to be written; I couldn't remain standing at *A Doll's House*; after Nora, Mrs Alving of necessity had to come' [v, p. 477]. *Ghosts* was a play that left no room for doubt, and its effect on contemporary Europe was quite explosive. Most leading critics in Scandinavia denounced the play (in Denmark only Georg Brandes defended it, and in Norway only Bjørnson and the feminists Camilla Collett and Amalie Skram). Thousands of copies of the text were returned to the publishers, and major theatres declined the option of mounting a production.

In *Ghosts* Ibsen at last abandoned the structure he had so far used in his modern social plays. He chose instead the retrospective, analytic structure of classical and neo-classic drama. The action begins only a matter of hours before the final catastrophe; the main concern of the play is to explore in retrospect the events, deeds and responses that have led up to the crisis. Ibsen was the first contemporary dramatist to make renewed use of an analytic structural pattern in his work, but the idea was clearly in the air at the time. In *Naturalism in the Theatre* (*Le naturalisme au théâtre*, 1881) Zola recommended it to contemporary dramatists in the same year *Ghosts* was published: 'I think we should go right back to neo-classic tragedy [. . .] to rediscover the simplicity of its action and its unique psychological and physical study of the characters'.

When we are first introduced to the various characters, some appear to be linked only by their social relationships, others by family ties. The main character, Mrs Helene Alving, is the widowed mistress of a large country estate called Rosenvold. The only character to whom she is clearly related through family ties is her son Osvald. However, as the action of the play unfolds, and successive layers of the past are stripped away, we see how a complex tissue of relationships binds her to her maid Regine and to Regine's father Engstrand. (He is the carpenter supervising the construction of an orphanage in memory of the late Captain Alving.) We also discover just how closely linked she is to the priest Manders.

Manders was the priest to whom Mrs Alving had once fled from her disastrous marriage. Although she had good reason to suspect that he was in love with her, he refused to offer her any support and insisted that she return to her husband. Whatever his personal feelings, Manders would never have risked offending public opinion by allowing himself to transgress conventionally accepted standards of behaviour.

Regine, we discover, is Captain Alving's illegitimate

daughter by a woman called Johanne who was at the time his wife's chambermaid at Rosenvold. As an act of charity, Mrs Alving took Regine into service after both Alving and Johanne had died. Engstrand was the man who accepted responsibility for Johanne's child, in return for the money given Johanne by Mrs Alving. Like his 'daughter', he does not know the identity of the real father.

When the action of the play takes place, Alving has been dead for ten years and Mrs Alving is now a middle-aged woman, still coming to terms with herself and all the painful memories of her past. The action begins with the arrival of Pastor Manders at Rosenvold to dedicate the orphanage in memory of the late Captain Alving. Osvald, now in his twenties and a successful artist in Paris, has returned home the previous evening. As these characters interact, unresolved conflicts are swiftly brought to the surface, old wounds are opened up again.

The setting for *Ghosts* is an elegant drawing room, with adjoining conservatory, in a Norwegian country house. In a letter he wrote in 1886 to Duke George of Meiningen, Ibsen described the kind of room he had in mind:

> The living-rooms of the oldest family seats of this type sometimes have dark coloured wall coverings. The lower halves of the walls are clad with simple wood panels. The ceilings, doors and window surrounds are treated in a similar fashion. The stoves are large, cumbersome and generally made of cast iron. The furniture is often *empire* in style; but the colours are consistently darker.

An elegant aristocratic setting in which the *empire* furniture not only signals the upper-class status of the Alvings but also contains a hint of French verve and *esprit*. The darker colours, however, are dictated by local taste.

A detailed examination of the stage directions shows that Ibsen made good use of his practical experience in the theatre in suggesting how the stage space should be used. Downstage areas are reserved for emotive scenes requiring close contact between actors and audience (as in the highly charged scenes between Osvald and Mrs Alving in Acts 2 and 3). Neutral discussions take place in the centre of the stage at or near a circular table with chairs around it; the area immediately downstage of the table is then available for use when characters get up from a discussion in an agitated frame of mind. The upstage area is used for dominant entrances and moments requiring particular focus (e.g. when Osvald makes his spectacular first entry smoking his father's pipe, or the poignant moment when Mrs Alving and Manders hear Osvald unwittingly emulating his father by attempting to kiss the maid in an adjoining room).

As in *A Doll's House*, Ibsen makes extensive use of visual symbolism in the action. The steady rain of the fjord landscape, frequently referred to in the dialogue, produces a leaden quality of lighting in Act 1 that is a visual correlative for the guilt-laden atmosphere at Rosenvold. The upstage conservatory, with its flowers and plants, provides a counterbalancing visual symbol of hope. It seems to represent for the different characters a focus for their longing for light. Significantly, it is Osvald and Regine who make most use of the area. At crucial moments in the action, lamps are lit in an attempt to dispel the chilling fog of misunderstandings in which the different characters are locked. At the end of Act 2, the orphanage burns down with a fierce red glow reflecting Osvald's state of mind at the time. Finally, in the closing moments of the play, a beautiful sunrise, mirroring the state of enlightenment Mrs Alving feels she has reached, is cruelly juxtaposed with

Osvald lapsing into madness and asking his mother for the sun, as he sits slumped in his chair.

There are important thematic symbols in the play. The orphanage can be seen as an embodiment of Mrs Alving's guilt at preserving the respectable façade of her disastrous marriage. When it burns down, Engstrand (who almost certainly set it alight) persuades Manders to use the residue of Alving's personal estate to help him establish a 'seamen's home' in town. What he has in mind is a sailors' brothel that will ironically be a far more fitting memorial to the late Captain Alving than an orphanage.

The ghosts of the title, as Mrs Alving makes clear in Act 2, are an expression, in symbolic terms, for the heritage of guilt burdening the major characters in the play. They are all of them fettered in their deeds and thoughts by a heritage of dead and useless ideals, beliefs, conditioned responses, and imprisoned in destructive patterns of interaction with each other. As Mrs Alving comments, they are all of them 'abysmally afraid of the light', afraid of change, afraid of acting freely and decisively.

Contrasted with the symbol of ghosts is the notion of *joie de vivre*, which Mrs Alving has never experienced since her decision to marry Alving for purely economic reasons and her subsequent insistence on duty and order as the only way to survive in her marriage. It is precisely this *joie de vivre* that Osvald has always longed for in his relationship with his mother and that, having failed to find it in his own life, he has attempted to capture in his paintings.

The central concern in *Ghosts* is the pattern of interaction between mother and son, which is explored in Acts 2 and 3. Mrs Alving desperately wishes to be a warm and supportive mother to her son whom she once bundled out of her home because of Alving's drunken and lecherous behaviour. All she wants now is to make up for the ten lost years that Osvald spent away from her by being a real mother to him. But she can only do that by treating Osvald as a dependent child rather than an adult. She even says to him at one point early in Act 3: 'I could almost bless this illness that drove you home to me' [v, p. 416].

As Osvald's behaviour takes on increasingly disturbing traits during the third and last act, Mrs Alving attempts to control his emotions by smothering him and forcing him into a pattern of behaviour she can manage. That is why she reveals the secret of Regine's parentage, effectively ruining the blossoming relationship between her son and her maid. Her instinctive response throughout Act 3 is to try and make Osvald revert to the role of a small child so that she can act out the mother's role (a role she once rejected) and sort out all his problems for him. Her very last speech to him sums up these aims: 'All these upsets have been too much for you. But now you'll be able to have a good long rest. At home, with your mother beside you, my darling. Anything you want you shall have, just like when you were a little boy. There now' [v, p. 421].

Osvald for his part feels chronically insecure as a result of his past and present relationship with his mother. At one and the same time she manages to make him feel unwanted and yet emotionally imprisoned. The result is that he feels burning resentment towards her, and as the play progresses his resentment takes on an increasingly ugly shape. It culminates in a fierce argument towards the end of Act 3 where he taunts his mother with images of his impending brain seizure and hysterically insists that his mother should take his life. Summing up long years of resentment, he screams at her: 'I never asked you for life. And what sort of a life is this you've given me? I don't want it! Take it back!' [v, p. 420].

At the end of the play Osvald is rendered helpless in

front of Mrs Alving's eyes; he succumbs to a brain seizure diagnosed by a Paris physician as the result of an inherited disease. Normally it is assumed that Ibsen was referring here to general paralysis of the insane, the tertiary stage of a syphilitic infection Osvald has inherited from his father. In this case, Mrs Alving is confronted by a horrifying image that encapsulates the consequences of her past deeds and compromises and her ultimate acceptance, however unwilling, of contemporary social prejudices.

An alternative, and in some ways even more terrifying, interpretation sees Mrs Alving herself as the major force unwittingly driving Osvald into madness. The evidence for this is in the dialogue. Repeatedly, Mrs Alving undermines her son's fragile sense of security and individuality. Time and again, she refuses to believe the implications of what he is saying. Her insistent attempts at imposing her vision on Osvald only serve to exacerbate his anguished state, driving him into a frenzy. According to this interpretation, Osvald eventually withdraws at the end of the play from his intolerable anxiety into a catatonic state of living death.[7] Whichever interpretation one accepts, Mrs Alving is left at the end of the play facing the dreadful consequences of her willingness to conform, and of her life-long attempt to impose order on disorder at whatever cost.

Ghosts was intended to raise profound issues about the nature of contemporary society and the way it affected the lives of individual men and women. Seemingly the balance between environmental determinism and human freedom has shifted decisively towards the sphere of determinism. But *Ghosts* is ultimately a play about human agency. The major characters are subject to enormous social and environmental pressures, but it is their deeds that forge a chain of destructive responses. They themselves create their own prisons of the heart and mind. Mrs Alving's decision to marry for purely economic reasons; Manders's rejection of her; her subsequent decision to return to her husband and keep up appearances; these are all decisive actions that in their turn engender a nexus of destructive responses. As Ibsen himself commented: 'Nemesis is invited upon the offspring by marrying for extrinsic reasons, even when they are religious or moral' [v, p. 467].

The social isolation in which the characters live makes it particularly difficult for them to break out of a destructive pattern of response. But although change is difficult, it is not impossible. Mrs Alving, for instance, has undergone a substantial change in attitude over the years, even in the isolation of Rosenvold. Unfortunately for her, she has not yet managed to change sufficiently to cope with the crisis confronting her in her relationship with Osvald.

During the course of the play, Mrs Alving makes a concerted attempt to come to terms with her past errors. She acknowledges that, in marrying Alving, she in effect sold herself like a common prostitute. She recognises that Manders, then as now, was far too much a willing prisoner of convention ever to be of any use to her. She accepts that her frigid rejection of Alving made his life a misery and probably drove him to the worst of his excesses. What she cannot yet accept is the fact that she herself blighted the life of her son by once rejecting him to keep up an acceptable façade at home. Nemesis is invited upon her son Osvald because of the emotional confusion in which he has lived since a child. And it is Mrs Alving who is in large measure responsible for that confusion.

In his preliminary notes for the play, Ibsen wrote: 'These women of the modern age, mistreated as daughters, as sisters, as wives, not educated in accordance with their talents, debarred from following their mission, deprived of their inheritance, embittered in mind – these are the ones who supply the mothers for the new generation. What will be the result?' [v, p. 468]. The play itself answered that question quite unequivocally. Contained within the fabric of patriarchal society were the seeds of confusion, alienation and even madness.

At the end of *Ghosts*, there is no tragic reconciliation, because the major characters have not yet achieved real insight into their dilemma. There is no moment of *anagnorisis* or recognition. Osvald has lapsed into madness, arguably the protective madness of catatonic withdrawal. Mrs Alving, in speechless terror, is confronted by the choice of giving her son the lethal morphine tablets he has requested or nursing him in his child-like state of madness. In this final silent tableau Ibsen provocatively expects his audience to supply the insight that has so far eluded the major characters. It is not a cathartic experience he offers but an emotional and intellectual challenge. (That is why he himself called the play, not a tragedy but a domestic drama.) *Ghosts* was written to provoke people into thought. As Ibsen commented in a letter to Otto Borchsenius in January 1882: 'It may very well be that this play is in a number of respects rather daring. But I thought the time had come when a few frontier posts ought to be moved' [v, p. 476].

'The Lady from the Sea'

Several years and plays later, when Ibsen returned to the theme of doll's house marriages in his play *The Lady from the Sea* (1888), his vision had grown less apocalyptic, softer, but also sadder. This play has none of the aggression or sense of outrage that inspired the writing of *Ghosts*: instead there is an almost elegiac sadness in the way Ibsen

1. H. P. Holst's production of *A Doll's House*, Theatre Royal, Copenhagen, 1879.

men.

Nº 41. (til Nº 9 [Hr. Meyer) Hørte De
      det? Det kan De have
      godt af! (Her maatt)

Nº 9 Han er ikke bange
      maa jg sige! (Her maatt
                    og gnider
                    sig i Hænderne)   (33)

Nº 8, 2 Hun var s'aa tydelig!

Nº 40,   }   Nº 32. – 28. }
   42.   } Aa – aa!   – 33. – 29. } Hysser.
   35.   }   – 30. –
   34   }   – 34.
   27.   }   Fru Stockmann kaster uroligt:

      Munslev overalt, indtil der
      ringes.*

(Nº 53. (den drukne Mand kommer
      ind fra Baggrundsdøren og
      baner sig Vej til Byfogdens
      Nærhed.

2. William Bloch's prompt-book notes for his production of *An Enemy of the People*, Theatre Royal, Copenhagen, 1883.

3. André Antoine's production of *The Wild Duck*, Théâtre Libre, Paris, 1891.

4. Gordon Craig's production of *Rosmersholm*, Florence, 1906.

5. Design sketch by Edvard Munch for Max Reinhardt's production of *Ghosts*, Kammerspiele, Berlin, 1906.

6. Johanne Dybwad as Rebecca West in her own production of *Rosmersholm*, National Theatre, Kristiania, 1922.

7. Ingmar Bergman's production of *Hedda Gabler*, Royal Dramatic Theatre,
   Stockholm, 1964.

8. Ingmar Bergman's production of *Hedda Gabler*, Royal Shakespeare
   Company, Aldwych Theatre, London, 1970.

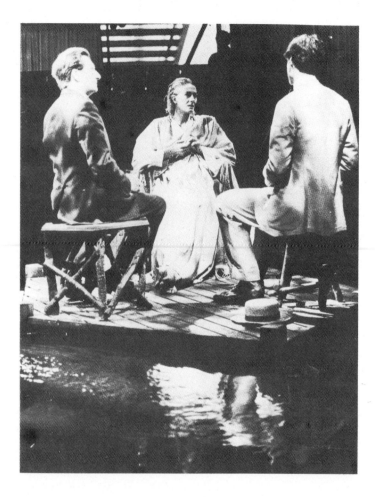

9. Michael Elliott's production of *The Lady from the Sea*, Royal Exchange Theatre, Manchester, 1978.

10. Peter Hall's production of *John Gabriel Borkman*, National Theatre, London, 1975.

11. John Barton's production of *Pillars of Society*, Royal Shakespeare Company, Aldwych Theatre, London, 1977.

12. The asylum scene in Peter Stein's production of *Peer Gynt*, Schaubühne am Halleschen Ufer, Berlin, 1971.

13. The final pietà image in Peter Stein's production of *Peer Gynt*, Schaubühne am Halleschen Ufer, Berlin, 1971.

describes the marriage of a widowed country doctor, Wangel, with his younger, second wife, Ellida.

As in Ibsen's earlier plays, there is a close relationship between the characters' attitudes and aspirations and the environment in which they live. Cut off and isolated as they are in a small fjord town, the characters are obliged to temper their personal and professional hopes to fit in with the fjord landscape in which they live. As the play opens, Ballested, a painter and tourist guide, is seen painting a picture of a mermaid languishing half-dead on a rock, cut off from the open sea. The inspiration for this motif came from Ellida who longs for the open sea; by comparison with the sea, the water in the fjord seems to her stale and brackish. So does her life. She and Wangel are like the sleepy carp who swim aimlessly around in their garden pond, while real life seems to pass them by, way beyond the horizon. It is late summer and soon their few contacts with the outside world will cease as winter closes in and the ice will come to block the entrance to the fjord. As Ellida herself comments in Act 3, the long summer days contain: 'a threat of the long dark days to come. And this threat casts its shadow over human joy . . . like a passing cloud that casts its shadow over the fjord. There it lay so bright and blue. Then all of a sudden . . .' [vii, p. 75].

In *The Lady from the Sea*, Ibsen has moved a long way from the oppressive social determinism of *Ghosts*. His characters now seem to wrestle with an almost metaphysical sense of determinism, a sense of the whole of creation being deeply flawed. Ibsen himself summed up this feeling in his preliminary notes for the play: 'Everywhere limitation. From this comes melancholy like a subdued song of mourning over the whole of human existence and all the activities of men' [vii, p. 449]. The play is filled with moments of sad beauty. It shows a world in which there is little scope for genuine fulfilment. The best that can be hoped for is to 'acclimatise oneself', as Ballested says, to the limitations imposed by the environment and by life itself. The alternative, illustrated by the example of the mermaid, is to languish and die.

This is the first of Ibsen's plays since *Brand* and *Peer Gynt* to be set predominantly out of doors (only one of the five acts takes place in a garden room). The play is dominated by nature imagery: vistas of the fjord and alpine peaks beyond; a vantage point high above the town; a shaded part of Wangel's garden with its carp pond; Ellida's leafy arbour. But the predominant image is that of water: the water in the sea, the fjord, the carp pond. For Ellida, the image of water sums up her longing to regress from the pain of human being to a less complex but more mystical form of being in the primeval sea.

When we first see Ellida and Wangel on stage in Act 1, it is clear that they have drifted into an untenable pattern of response. Ellida is suffering from a severe depression, exacerbated by her lack of a fulfilled relationship with her husband and his two daughters from his previous marriage, Bolette and Hilde. She only copes by taking drugs given her by Wangel. He, for his part, cannot understand her depression or her refusal to sleep with him and turns to heavy drinking. Wangel tries to break this deadlock by inviting Arnholm, a teacher and an old friend of Ellida's, to come and visit them. Arnholm's arrival in Act 1 has the desired effect of breaking up this destructive stasis, as Ellida begins to reveal to him some of her secret worries.

Wangel wisely builds on Arnholm's intervention and, in Act 2, probes the reasons for Ellida's depression. It seems that it began some three years earlier when she lost a baby. She started to have nightmarish fantasies about a lover whom she felt she had betrayed, a mysterious seaman,

possibly a murderer, to whom she had symbolically betrothed herself. In her obsessional state, she became
convinced that her dead child's eyes were those of the
seaman. That is why she refused to sleep with Wangel.

The immediate effect of this confession is an intensifica-
tion of Ellida's emotional crisis, which leads directly in Act
3 to the conjuring up of the vision from her past that both
terrifies and attracts her. It is as if she projects on to the
stage, from the depths of her own fears, the image of the
mysterious seaman who represents for her both salvation
and damnation. Arguably, in Act 3 with the arrival of the
seaman on the last tourist boat of the season, the action of
the play moves completely into the sphere of Ellida's
dreams and fantasies so that now, as in an expressionist
dream play, we see everything through her eyes, including
the responses of the other characters.

Wangel, for instance, reacts initially as Ellida would
expect him to. In Act 3, he attempts to assume
authoritarian control over events, dismissing the claims of
the Stranger as pure fantasy and threatening to call the
police. It is not until Act 4, when the image of the Stranger
has receded from the forefront of Ellida's consciousness,
that she and Wangel talk through their crisis, exploring
even the most painful issues.

What emerges from this discussion as the root cause of
Ellida's unhappiness is the fact that she feels robbed of her
essential freedom as a human being. As she sees it, she
allowed Wangel to come and buy her in marriage, which
has left her feeling soiled and tainted. That is why she tries
to wash herself clean every day in the waters of the fjord. At
first, Wangel fails to understand the point she is making. He
still insists on asserting his authority as husband and doctor,
telling his wife that she is not fit enough to choose between
her married life with him and an uncertain future with the

mysterious seaman. But in a last traumatic confrontation with the Stranger in Act 5, when Ellida relives the worst of her fears and her temptations, Wangel finally gives her complete freedom to choose, but freedom with responsibility. In relinquishing any claim to have authority over her, he gives her incontrovertible proof of his affection for her. At that point, Ellida is able to choose him for the first time in complete freedom and, in so doing, is able to see how she might in future relate more openly and genuinely to Wangel's two daughters.

The play closes on this note of reconciliation, but any happiness is tinged with more than a hint of sadness. Ellida has indeed freely chosen the path of duty, but in so doing she denies the validity of her longings for a more expansive, romantic freedom, what Wangel calls her 'craving for the unattainable . . . for the limitless, for the infinite . . .' [vii, p. 120].

To underline the point, Ibsen shows us Wangel's eldest daughter, Bolette, swallowing any romantic dreams she may once have had when she agrees in Act 5 to marry the prematurely ageing Arnholm. He at least offers her the prospect of travel abroad and is effectively her only hope of escaping from the limitations of her environment: 'Imagine! To be free . . . and to be able to travel. And not to have to worry about the future. Not to have these stupid worries about having to make ends meet . . .' [vii, p. 115]. Just like her stepmother, Bolette has little option but to sell herself in marriage when she is made an acceptable offer.

At the end of the play, Ballested the painter reminds us that mermaids languish and die away from the freedom of the sea, but men and women (and particularly women) can and must 'acclimatise themselves', must learn to conform, if they wish to remain sane. Ellida regains her sanity, but has she lost something vital in the process? The ending of the play is sufficiently ambiguous to be susceptible to a wide variety of interpretations.

Perhaps the real strength of the play lies in its poetic evocation of a transient late summer warmth before the darkness of winter returns. Ballested reminds us of this very image in the closing lines of the play: 'Soon the seaways are all locked, as the poet says. How sad, Mrs Wangel!' [vii, p. 123]. There is an undeniable beauty in Ellida's reconciliation with Wangel, but it is tinged with sadness and hedged around with question marks. Although the play does reassert the values of freedom and responsibility, it does so against a backcloth of elegiac renunciation. The effect is not unlike that produced by the ending of Racine's *Bérénice*. With its evocation of a bitter-sweet, late summer mood, *The Lady from the Sea* was to occupy a unique position in the canon of Ibsen's plays. His two late plays that explore the theme of doll's house marriages introduce us to increasingly icy relationships where the warmth of an August sun is long forgotten.

'Hedda Gabler'

In his next play, *Hedda Gabler* (1890), autumn has come. Hedda, the main character in the play, feels an autumnal chill in her soul as she looks out at the yellow, withered leaves in her garden. It is 'already September', and the darkness of winter is now disturbingly close. Hedda is married to a promising but boring academic called Jørgen Tesman. The man whose company she most enjoys, Judge Brack, is a polished but ruthless pragmatist who brilliantly manipulates social conventions to his own advantage. Ejlert Løvborg is a former admirer of Hedda's. He is a gifted but unstable genius, given to heavy drinking, who has since been tamed by Thea Elvsted, a woman who was at school with Hedda. These are the major characters, all linked either socially or through bonds of friendship, who act out Ibsen's tragi-comedy.

At times the action is closer to black farce than tragedy. In his preliminary notes for the play, Ibsen anticipates this mood in a brief description he gives of Hedda's state of mind: 'Life for Hedda resolves itself as a farce that isn't "worth seeing through to the end" ' [vii, p. 486]. And this farcical quality that she sees in life colours everything said and done in the play, reducing even the most poetic ideals to a mockery of themselves. During the action serious things are transacted, and eventually both Løvborg and Hedda die. The potential wasted in these two deaths is clearly tragic in substance. But the manner of their deaths and the reaction their deaths produce in others are essentially comic.

The predominantly comic tone of the play is reinforced by a simple linear structure. In contrast to *Ghosts*, where characters probe each other and their past in order to lay bare their real motives, *Hedda Gabler* moves swiftly forward in time in a linear manner and with only the briefest of glimpses into the past. Even the dialogue is compressed and taut, as in all comic writing. There are virtually no speeches longer than three or four lines, and there are frequent passages of almost pure comic repartee. Structurally, each act builds to a climactic situation to which Hedda then reacts.

At the end of Act 1 Hedda finds herself faced by the threat of social regression implicit in Tesman's possible failure to obtain a professorial appointment; this would at a stroke take away the one thing that made her marriage to Tesman feasible in the first place. Hedda reacts to this prospect by reaching for her father's pistols. At the end of Act 2, Hedda's successful intervention in Løvborg's relationship with Thea, culminating in the 'reformed' Løvborg's departure for Brack's bacchic feast, fills Hedda with such elation that she feels like burning off Thea's hair.

At the end of Act 3, Løvborg takes his leave of Hedda, broken in spirit, having lost the manuscript of his new book, and socially in disgrace after his drunken and disorderly behaviour following Brack's party. He accepts the gift Hedda presses on him of one of General Gabler's pistols, leaving her with the feeling that he will die nobly and beautifully like a true aristocrat. Hedda reacts to this situation by venting her most destructive feelings on the relationship Løvborg and Thea had established. She burns Thea's 'child', the manuscript of the book Løvborg wrote under Thea's calming influence. By the end of Act 4, Hedda realises that Thea and her own husband Tesman will exclude her from any participation in the work of piecing together Løvborg's manuscript. Hedda also realises that Brack, fully aware that it was she who gave Løvborg his suicide weapon, now has her in his power. Feeling trapped and rejected at one and the same time, she shoots herself in a gesture of almost petulant defiance. Throughout the play, the seriousness of the things she does is in some measure offset by the incongruity of her various responses. She reacts rather like an angry child to the various problems confronting her. Finally even her suicide is a childish gesture in which she thumbs her defiance at a world she neither understands nor likes.

During the first three acts of the play, Hedda exercises a decisive influence over the way the stage space is structured and used. She decides where to place the furniture and also where the different characters will sit. In Act 2, for instance, she cleverly directs Brack and Tesman to use her upstage room for punch and cigars so that she can use the drawing-room for her encounter with Løvborg. In all three acts she bullies Thea into sitting or standing in positions where she can dominate her. In Act 4, however, this changes drastically. As the consequences of her actions become known – the destruction of Ejlert's manuscript and his subsequent death – she loses her previously dominant status. While the others literally pick up the shattered pieces of what she has destroyed, she finds herself treated like the irresponsible child she has become.

Visually, she is politely but firmly ousted from every corner of the stage. First, Tesman and Thea invade her private room upstage to start piecing together Ejlert's notes. Next, they take over her escritoire because the light is not good enough in the little room. When Hedda moves to her corner by the stove downstage, and sits on one of the stools, Brack stands over her menacingly, quietly making oblique sexual threats. Even when she retreats to her room again and draws the curtains to shut the others out, she cannot do as she wants. She attempts to play the piano but is immediately told to be quiet. There is literally no space left for her. Very carefully, Ibsen has prepared us in visual terms for the inevitable shot that finally rings out.

The problem around which the play is structured is similar to that of *Ghosts*. Hedda has allowed herself to become trapped in a pointless conventional marriage. Like Mrs Alving, she finds it is not so easy to escape, having once taken such a decisive step. Hedda's reasons were partly financial, partly social and psychological. Brought up as if she were a general's son by her father, she has acquired the arrogance and aspirations of the men of her class, without any hope of fulfilling them as a far from wealthy woman in a male-dominated society. She has no professional skills and cannot hope to remain a débutante for ever. It therefore seemed to her that marriage was the only avenue open to her. She avoided the ruthless men of her own class, such as

Judge Brack, and instead chose a docile academic as her husband, a man she could easily manage but who would serve his purpose by offering her some social status and prestige.

Unfortunately, things do not work out quite as Hedda planned. Life with Jørgen Tesman threatens to be boring and socially disadvantageous. The gulf between her hopes and the actual marriage in which she is imprisoned is brought home to her when the Tesmans are visited in Act 2 by Ejlert Løvborg. Hedda was once in love with Løvborg but was too cowardly, too afraid of scandal, to admit it. The sight of Løvborg in her own drawing room brings alive a painful image of what life might have been for her. Some of the bacchic intoxication implicit in that image is summed up in a vision she articulates of Løvborg with vineleaves in his hair. For her he represents spontaneity and creative genius: a life shared with him would have been very different from the future she faces as the wife of Jørgen Tesman.

Together on stage, under the watchful eyes of Judge Brack, Løvborg and Hedda exude a suppressed sexuality that is potentially explosive. Both of them are now trapped: Hedda in her doll's house marriage and Løvborg in his relationship with Thea. Unlike Mrs Alving, Hedda makes no attempt to understand how and why she is trapped. Instead she lashes out in sheer frustration, venting her spite on Løvborg, for what might have been, and on Thea, for daring to ensnare her man.

By the end of the play, Hedda has burnt the manuscript of Løvborg's new book, has driven her former hero to commit suicide, sees her husband responding warmly to Thea Elvsted and finds herself in the hands of Judge Brack who knows enough about her deeds to blackmail her into sleeping with him. Hedda's doll's house has turned into an emotional chamber of horrors.

Hedda Gabler is a cool, almost icy play. Even the laughter it provokes in production is at times sardonic. Like *Ghosts*, it is written to be deliberately provocative. It offers no tragic catharsis. What it leaves an audience with is a feeling of waste. There is potential and idealism in Hedda, but no outlet for it in contemporary society. (As Ibsen himself commented in his preliminary notes: 'With Hedda, there is poetry deep down'.) Brought up to be ashamed of her own sex, deeply imbued with a fear of scandal, Hedda cannot find a viable means of expressing her desire for personal freedom and fulfilment. Her real longing, as Ejlert rightly suspected, was for a life in which there could be authenticity, truth and genuine reciprocity, in which there could be intellectual, emotional and sexual fulfilment without subterfuge and shame. Given the repressive values of her upbringing and social environment, such a life seems to her an impossible dream. Instead she chooses a conventional solution, allowing herself to be imprisoned in the kind of shallow marriage of convenience that was typical of the age. The result is a disaster for all concerned.

All that remains at the end of the play is the comic incongruity of Brack's and Tesman's response to her suicide:

TESMAN (*shouts at Brack*): She shot herself! Shot herself in the head! Just think!
BRACK (*half-paralysed in the armchair*): But, good God! People don't do such things!

Their shocked response summed up an age when women were expected to conform to the written and unwritten rules of a patriarchal society.

By underlining the precise social factors contributing to Hedda's distressing psychological state, Ibsen made it clear that what happened to Hedda was neither inevitable nor pre-ordained. Nor was she simply an abnormal personality, as some contemporary critics assumed. Her actions are perfectly intelligible, even if emotionally immature and destructive, responses to the extreme pressures confronting her in the ruthless, male-dominated world in which she lives. Underneath the laughter in this tragi-comedy, Ibsen spelled out with almost icy clarity the price to be paid, in terms of human misery and suffering, for living in Hedda's world. Through the use of laughter, its appeal was to the mind as well as to the heart. It was written, as was *Ghosts*, with the conscious aim of challenging its audiences to reassess the value structures underpinning their society.

'John Gabriel Borkman'

In *John Gabriel Borkman* (1896), the last of Ibsen's plays concentrating on the theme of doll's house marriages, the icy grip of winter totally pervades the whole play. Right from the opening stage directions, the setting mirrors almost expressionistically the spiritual state of the protagonists. The play moves from the stuffy, faded splendour of Mrs Borkman's sitting-room to the icy grandeur of a Norwegian winter landscape, with its dark pine trees and deep snow.

In structural terms, the analytic probing of past deeds and responses is counterbalanced by the forward-moving action of the play. The retrospective analysis concentrates on exploring the betrayals and disappointments in the triadic relationship between John Gabriel Borkman, his wife Gunhild and her twin sister Ella Rentheim. The main body of the action shows these three characters vying with each other to control the life and destiny of Borkman's son

Erhart. All three fail, when Erhart insists on living his own life with his wealthy mistress, Fanny Wilton.

Acts 1 and 2 concentrate on exploring the past. Act 3 and the beginning of Act 4 trace out the forward-moving action. The last section of Act 4 is a quiet coda in which the three major characters finally achieve insight into the way they have lived and accept the consequences of their past deeds. As Ella and Gunhild join hands over the dead body of the man they both loved, there is a genuine sense of recognition and reconciliation. Ibsen at last offers his audience an emotionally rounded catharsis.

In thematic terms, the play is Ibsen's final reckoning with the destructive values and assumptions of contemporary bourgeois society, with the world of Consul Bernick and Torvald Helmer. There are many striking parallels between Bernick and Borkman. Both are fired by dreams of power and glory. Both regard women as interchangeable and betray the woman they love for the sake of material advantage. Both end up believing their own rhetoric. But where Bernick, by sheer chance, escaped the disastrous consequences of his actions, we learn in the retrospective action how Borkman fell victim to his dreams. He speculated with money and shares he did not own until his whole empire was brought crashing down. After a lengthy prison sentence, Borkman has lived for eight years at home, pacing up and down his room like a caged wolf, never once seeing or speaking to his embittered wife Gunhild.

In the first two acts of the play, we learn a great deal about the contrasting characters of Gunhild and her twin sister Ella. Gunhild had once fought her sister for the hand of John Gabriel. Not because she loved him, as Ella did, but because she was ambitious and impressed with his flair. Gunhild consciously married a man who would bring her fame and wealth. She became an archetypal doll wife, revelling in the reflected glory that came her way because of her husband. She spent lavishly and encouraged her husband to be even more extravagant than he was by nature. But when he failed her and was arrested, she rejected him completely. Gunhild is a woman completely imprisoned within the value structures of the doll's house. Just as she once basked vicariously in Borkman's glory, she now loathes the sense of shame and dishonour he has brought upon the family and is determined to restore the family name with the help of her son Erhart.

Ella is far less rigid, far less willing to allow her responses to be determined by social convention. She was once a loving and spontaneous woman who could have offered Borkman the kind of warmth and support he never found with Gunhild. Even in adversity, she claims in Act 2, she would have stood by him. But Borkman dismissed her because of his vaulting ambition, and from then on her life has been a desert. The confrontation between these two characters in Act 2 culminates with powerful statements summing up their fundamentally divergent responses to life:

ELLA RENTHEIM: You have killed love in me. (*Goes closer to him.*) Do you understand what that means? The Bible speaks of a mysterious sin for which there is no forgiveness. I have never understood before what that could be. Now I do understand. The great sin for which there is no forgiveness is to murder love in a human soul. [. . .]

BORKMAN: But you must remember that I am a man. As a woman, you were the most precious thing in the world to me. But in the last resort, one woman can always be replaced by another ... [. . .] I wanted to gain command of all the sources of power in this land.

> Earth, mountain, forest, and sea – I wanted control of
> all their resources. I wanted to build myself an empire,
> and thereby create prosperity for thousands and
> thousands of others.   [viii, pp. 197–8]

In these few lines, Ibsen expresses an unusually passionate
critique of the acquisitive, materialist values of contemporary society. Invoking one of Christ's darker sermons in
Matthew 12: vv. 31–2, he equates Borkman's betrayal of
Ella for the sake of the power and the glory with the
terrifying sin against the Holy Spirit, the one sin for which
there is no forgiveness. The resonant quality of the image
adds an almost mythic stature to this clash between one
character who represents the unconditional demands of
love and human commitment and the other character who
personifies all the flawed materialist values of a fallen
world.

Borkman dies a victim to his dreams, hopelessly imprisoned within his vision of the power and the glory. But even
he acknowledges in Act 4 that he will never enter his
kingdom because he once killed the potential for love in
Ella Rentheim. This brief moment of recognition immediately precedes his death, which he describes as a hand of
iron clutching his heart. All that remains is the ghostly
reconciliation of the twin sisters over the corpse of the man
who helped to ruin their lives.

In this play of icy landscapes and broken lives, Ibsen has
placed a contrasting image of warmth and gaiety, in the
figure of Fanny Wilton, one of the most sensuously
attractive women characters he ever drew. At her first
appearance in Act 1, he described her as: 'a shapely and
strikingly beautiful woman in her thirties; generous, smil-
ing red lips; sparkling eyes; rich, dark hair' [viii, p. 171].
Amidst all the suffering and havoc caused by the patriar-

chal conventions of contemporary society, she represents a vivacious image of liberated *joie de vivre*. Divorced from her husband, she is a woman whose earlier sufferings have hardened and tempered her personality. She is hard-headed, defensively ironic in manner and quite capable of looking after herself. She is also wealthy enough to enjoy considerable freedom in a materialistic society. Despite her hard-headedness, she is still able to envisage a relationship involving warmth and happiness. She finds this with Erhart, but is perfectly aware that it is unlikely to last for ever, in view of his youth and immaturity. Hence her decision to take a younger woman, Frida Foldal, with her on her journey South with Erhart. Frida will be someone for Erhart 'to fall back on' when he and Mrs Wilton have tired of each other.

Mrs Wilton represents a clear alternative to the subservient doll wives of earlier plays. In contrast to the other women in Ibsen's plays who have suffered a first disastrous marriage (Mrs Linde in *A Doll's House* and Mrs Sørby in *The Wild Duck*), she no longer believes in stable and lasting relationships. But like these other women, she has learnt how to cope from her past misfortunes and how to accept responsibility for her actions. Given her exceptional wealth, she does not offer an ideal model for the dependent wives Ibsen shows trapped in their various dolls' houses. But her complete lack of bitterness and her willing acceptance of whatever life brings, whether happiness or loneliness, make her an attractively warm personality.

It was entirely fitting that in this, his final reckoning with the repressive marriages he had depicted in his mature work, Ibsen should also depict an alternative, liberated vision of life. While Borkman dies a prisoner of his dreams, and while Gunhild acknowledges how coldness of heart killed both her and her sister long ago, Erhart and Fanny

Wilton fly South, to the warmth of a relationship based on mutual honesty and freedom.

In *John Gabriel Borkman*, far more obviously than in many of his mature plays, Ibsen shows characters making clear and decisive choices that shape the pattern of their lives. Borkman consciously chooses to sacrifice love for ambition and subsequently chooses to remain a prisoner of his materialistic dreams. Erhart chooses to break with his parents, although they subject him to remorseless emotional blackmail. Mrs Wilton chooses her life style, despite the disapproval of contemporary society. Gunhild and Ella both choose their differing values and patterns of behaviour and both choose to be reconciled after Borkman's death. There are powerful social and psychological pressures at work in the play, but nevertheless the different characters all unmistakably choose their own fate.

The juxtaposition of social determinism with individual freedom and responsibility runs like a leitmotiv through Ibsen's mature work. At times his major characters are so fettered by the pressures of determinism that they remain confused or embittered in their responses. In these cases, Ibsen challenges his audiences to supply the insight and the positive vision that eludes such characters. However, in *John Gabriel Borkman* the whole play is a resounding and unequivocal reaffirmation of human agency, freedom and responsibility. It was a fitting climax to his work as a social dramatist.

If one looks back over the whole spectrum of Ibsen's plays dealing with modern social and marital problems, one finds that the role of women in them is consistently used as a yardstick for judging the maturity and humanity of contemporary society. For the most part, Ibsen's judgement is a negative one. As he saw it, women were a disadvantaged group in the repressive patriarchal world of late nineteenth-century Europe. A number of his major women characters struggle, with varying degrees of success, to achieve sufficient insight to liberate themselves from the fetters of social and psychological determinism that bind them. Others react neurotically or destructively to the pressures that threaten them in their social or personal interaction. Only a handful achieve a measure of genuine fulfilment, and all of these have suffered a previous disastrous marriage or relationship.

Although he does not attack the notion of marriage in itself in his plays (even if the ideal of marriage articulated by Dina Dorf in *Pillars of Society* seems increasingly distant in his late plays), what causes him deep concern is the lack of genuine reciprocity in the conventional marriages of his day. Ironically, in the last of his social plays, it is only a wealthy divorcee, with the financial freedom to flout social convention, who can claim any kind of authenticity in her relationships with men.

Using techniques ranging from serious debate to ironic juxtaposition, from provocative and at times sardonic laughter to emotional catharsis, Ibsen's consistent aim in these social plays was to explore the problems and anxieties of contemporary men and women in their historical context, in order to help audiences to understand the nature of and the reasons for the suffering of the different characters. In so doing, he achieved precisely the kind of progressive 'break-through' in drama of which Georg Brandes had dreamt in the early 1870s. He also provided a fertile source of inspiration for socially committed playwrights ranging from Shaw to Arthur Miller. Even today, a modern British playwright like David Hare can think of no better definition of the role of the social dramatist than the one Ibsen had already given in his plays: 'We are drawing close, I think to what a playwright can do.

He can put people's sufferings in a historical context; and by doing that, he can help to explain their pain'.[8]

This, it seems to me, is why plays like *A Doll's House* or *Hedda Gabler* can speak to us across the barriers of time and space as immediately as when they were first written. The controversy may have faded: the representation of 'human beings, human moods and human destinies, seen against a background of contemporary social conditions and attitudes'[9] remains as fresh as ever.

5
Symbolist Plays

In his various social plays, Ibsen had repeatedly explored how far individual responses were shaped or fettered by social determinism, how far social existence could be seen to determine consciousness. However, beginning with *The Wild Duck* in 1884, Ibsen wrote a series of plays in the 1880s and 1890s in which there is a subtle but distinct shift of emphasis from the social to the personal. In *Rosmersholm* (1886), *The Master Builder* (1892), *Little Eyolf* (1894) and *When we dead awaken* (1899), complex personal relationships are explored within an overall framework of symbolism or myth. In these symbolist plays, the various characters are still carefully located within a specific social environment that shapes their pattern of living and, to some extent, their attitudes. But the author's major concern is no longer the relationship between the characters and their environment but rather the intensity and complexity of their inter-personal relationships. In these plays, the pain or suffering of the characters is not fully intelligible because it is seen in its social and historical context. Instead, the characters themselves, in the way they interact, largely determine their own fate.

Ibsen explores in his symbolist plays the politics of personal relationships (the strategies people adopt to achieve dominant, submissive or complementary roles in their relationships with each other). Repeatedly, he contrasts love and violence: authentic, unselfish love that accepts others for what they are and emotional violence that tries to coerce others into submissive behaviour. Ibsen shows repeatedly how manipulative emotional violence is usually unacknowledged and often uses the signs and language of love in a way that is confusing and disabling.

'The Wild Duck'

In his early jottings for *The Wild Duck* in 1883, Ibsen suggests a play that will explore a variety of social and political issues, including dreams of a socialist revolution, women's role in society, marriage, and the political rights of the majority versus the minority. When he began work on the play in earnest in April 1884, he was no longer concerned with these social and political issues. The focus of his attention had shifted towards the politics of family life. He made this quite clear in a letter to his publisher in June 1884: 'The play does not touch on political or social problems, or indeed any matters of public import. It takes place entirely within the confines of family life. I dare say it will arouse some discussion; but it cannot offend anyone' [Meyer, pp. 548–9].

The thrust of the action grows from the meeting between two men: a rich man's son, Gregers Werle, and Hjalmar Ekdal, who has come down in the world through family disgrace. Many years ago, these two were close friends and their fathers were business associates. However, Old Ekdal was convicted of felling trees on state property and had to serve a term in prison. Meanwhile Old Werle has prospered. Around this meeting between two former friends, Ibsen builds a play in which the contrast between two social classes – symbolised in the figures of the rich merchant Werle and the broken, impoverished Old Ekdal – is less important than the politics of family life explored in both social environments.

Structurally, the play follows a fast-moving comic pattern, reminiscent of classic or neo-classic comedy. In Act 1, Hjalmar has been invited to a sumptuous dinner party at Old Werle's by his former friend, Gregers Werle. The introductory, expository nature of this act is put to comic effect in Act 2 when Hjalmar, having returned from the dinner party, embroiders his account of what happened there to the point where the various humiliations he suffered are turned into personal triumphs. The gauche social misfit we saw in Act 1, who even denied his own father out of embarrassment, becomes in his own words a suave debonair man of the world who told all the Chamberlains present a thing or two. This is comic irony of the kind one finds in Jonson, Molière and Holberg. Acts 3 to 5 depend for their comic effect on the various interventions of Gregers Werle into the life of the Ekdal family. Gregers brings with him an abstract claim of the ideal, a ready formulated image of authentic existence, that he tries to impose on his old friend Hjalmar, on Hjalmar's wife Gina and on their adolescent daughter Hedvig. He fails because these various people simply cannot live up to his *a priori* ideal. In the case of Hjalmar and Gina, the failure is comic. In the case of Hedvig, it is tragic and leads to her suicide.

The play is shot through with visual and verbal symbolism. The central symbol, the wild duck of the title, is a bird that Old Werle brought down on one of his hunting expeditions. It was wounded and dived below the water, biting itself fast in the weeds, from where it was rescued by one of Werle's gun dogs. Now Hedvig nurses it in the loft. Hjalmar and Old Ekdal are both likened to the wounded duck that dived down below the surface to hide (and Gregers would like to be the clever dog who retrieves Hjalmar), but it is Hedvig who feels most at one with the wild duck. Unlike Nina in Chekhov's *The Seagull*, who claims to be a seagull, Hedvig never actually claims to be a wild duck. But the words she uses in Act 3 to describe the bird apply equally to her: 'She's completely cut off from her friends. And then everything about the wild duck is so mysterious. Nobody really knows her; and nobody knows where she's from either' [vi, p. 182]. Hedvig, like the wild duck, has also been down in the ocean depths. That is what she calls her fantasy playground in the loft. There life takes on an entirely different dimension. It is a place of magic that can transport her across time and continents. Although there are still symbols of death in the loft – its contents were once owned by a seaman nicknamed 'The flying Dutchman' and there is Harrison's *History of London* with its engraving of death and the maiden (an image prefiguring her own fate) – somehow even death takes on another hue in the magic atmosphere of the place.

For Old Ekdal, the loft, with its withered Christmas trees, its tame rabbits and chickens, represents the mighty forest at Højdal, teeming with game. His 'hunting' expeditions in the loft, when he shoots the occasional rabbit for supper, remind him of his former life as an intrepid bear hunter in the forests. Both images, the ocean depths and the forests, are symbols of regression, representing an unvoiced longing on the part of the characters concerned to escape from the limitations of real life and regress to a less complex, less painful mode of being. But the ocean and the forests are potent forces that can both sustain and destroy. By the end of the play, the forests avenge themselves on Old Ekdal, as he himself comments, and the ocean depths claim Hedvig as their innocent victim.

The symbol of blindness recurs throughout the play. Hedvig is slowly going blind, but she has true insight into people's feelings. By way of contrast, Gregers is certain that he sees and speaks only the truth, but he is blind to reality because he can only see the world through the embittered eyes of his long-dead mother. Old Werle, like Hedvig, is likewise losing his sight. However, he is a pragmatist who proceeds to make sensible arrangements for his future. He decides to marry his housekeeper, Mrs Sørby, who will care for him in his blindness. In Act 1, the guests at his dinner party try to play blind man's buff with Mrs Sørby, but she is a woman who has hidden nothing from Werle about her past and he too has talked freely of his earlier life, including his affairs with Gina and other women. Despite his blindness and despite the past, they can face a future together, based on mutual understanding.

In terms of the stage setting, there is a striking contrast between the opulence of Werle's house in Act 1 and the Ekdals' garret in the remainder of the play. And yet both environments are warm and convivial. Werle is a man who enjoys power and who revels in being in the centre of things. It is hardly fortuitous therefore that his study should be located mid-way between his glittering reception rooms, seen upstage, and his offices stage left that are approached through a green baize door. His study is an attractive room, with an open fire and comfortable arm chairs. Hjalmar is ill at ease in this environment and moves around the stage in some embarrassment, particularly when his father shuffles in from Werle's offices. In the important encounter that takes place between Gregers and Old Werle in the latter part of the act, Gregers seeks out the fire (as he does later in Hjalmar's home). He needs the warmth and glow of the fire because of the chill he feels within him.

The setting for Acts 2 to 5 is a garret that Ibsen describes as 'threadbare but cosy'. Gina has a gift for creating a sense of cosy domesticity even in the midst of poverty. A grouping of sofa, table and chairs stage left is the focal point of the family's social life. That is where they work, eat, and entertain any visitors. Frequently, work is pushed aside to make way for food: beer and sandwiches, coffee and sandwiches, a generous lunch. Hjalmar lives for his food and Gina does her best to keep him well-fed and contented. Upstage centre, in a focal position, two large sliding doors conceal the entrance to the loft, a place of magic in which Old Ekdal, Hjalmar and Hedvig play like young children, while Gina, without complaint, does the work. When Hjalmar feels relaxed, as he does for most of the time in Acts 2 to 3, he either sits at the table or disappears into the loft to play. From the beginning of Act 4, however, when Gregers has 'opened his eyes' to the actual state of affairs in his home, he tends to pace around the stage in histrionic agitation.

Throughout the work, the lighting plays an important part, as Ibsen himself commented in a letter to the Christiania Theatre in November 1884: 'Also the lighting has significance; it is different for each act and is calculated to correspond to the mood that leaves its own special mark on each of the five acts' [vi, p. 440]. In Act 1, Werle's study is softly lit by green-shaded lamps, in contrast to the upstage reception room that is brilliantly lit. In his own quarters, Werle adjusts the lighting to the level he can tolerate. And in subtextual terms, he would in any case prefer to avoid too much harsh light being shed on his personal and business life. At the beginning of Act 2 we see a warm and attractive image of the Ekdal home, lit by a shaded lamp on the table. Gina and Hedvig talk happily together about domestic matters. Later in the act, when the doors upstage centre are opened to the loft, we see romantic moonlight streaming into the loft and understand at once why the loft has such magic appeal for Hedvig.

In Act 3 it is morning, and warm daylight floods through the large upstage skylight. This is an act in which we see the happy everyday life of the Ekdals, culminating in a noisy lunch for their friends Relling and Molvik. At the end of the act Gregers quite intentionally destroys this warmth. In Act 4, the sun is about to set and it is getting dark. Gregers has now cast his chill and shadow over the Ekdal household by telling Hjalmar about Gina's earlier affair with Old Werle. Unable to face up to all he has learnt about Gina's past, Hjalmar has been out all night drinking himself unconscious with Relling. When he finally returns, he selfishly rejects Hedvig because he suspects she may be Werle's illegitimate daughter. The effect this has on her is quite terrifying. Act 5 takes place in the cold blue-grey light of morning with wet snow lying on the panes of the skylight. In this cold grey dawn, the consequences of Gregers's interference are exposed with harsh, merciless inevitability. The ice in his heart, prompting all he says and does, is mirrored in the wet snow lying on the skylight windows. Because of Gregers, Hedvig dies.

What is it that makes Gregers so lethal? In his notes for the play, Ibsen suggests that Gregers is a man who knows and feels the deepest sorrows of childhood: 'family sorrows – painful home circumstances' [vi, p. 434]. In Act 1, his vitriolic discussion with his father leaves no doubt as to the reasons for those feelings:

WERLE: Gregers, I don't think there's any man in the world you hate as much as me.

GREGERS (*quietly*): I have seen you at too close quarters.

WERLE: You have seen me with your mother's eyes. (*Drops his voice a little.*) But you mustn't forget that those eyes were . . . clouded, now and again.

GREGERS (*trembling*): I understand what you are getting at. But who bears the blame for my mother's unhappy disability? It's you, and all these . . . ! The last of them was this female who was palmed off on Hjalmar Ekdal when you no longer . . . ugh! [vi, p. 149]

As Werle correctly points out, Gregers is still his mother's son. He has no identity beyond that. He can only see his father through his mother's eyes as a man so utterly ruthless he rode roughshod over those closest to him in order to achieve his personal ambitions. In his view, it was Werle's womanising and irresponsibly selfish behaviour that turned his mother into a neurotic and later an alcoholic wreck, driving her finally to an early grave. Even as a child he took his mother's part. It never occurred to him to see the way his mother's constant recriminations and hysterical self-indulgence drove Werle into the arms of other women. Now his childhood responses have hardened into emotional fetters from which he can find no release. In Gregers's case, the politics of family life in a house dominated by an unyieldingly authoritarian father and a mother who responded with violent emotional blackmail have left him so incurably wounded, so damaged, that he can only succeed in relating destructively to others, when he desperately wants to bring new life and hope.

The Ekdals, by way of contrast, have established a warm and viable pattern of family life. From what we see of Gina and Hjalmar in Acts 2 and 3, it is clear that they have adopted perfectly complementary roles in relation to each other. Gina may have lured Hjalmar into marriage because she was pregnant. But she has since run his home and his photography business efficiently and without complaint. She is prosaic and hardworking where Hjalmar is the sensitive romantic. He is also a lazy parasite who prefers to sleep and daydream rather than work, but with his blarney and his flute, he provides the sparkle and the fun in the home. Hedvig binds them together with her naïvely loving commitment to them both. She is a bond of peace. There is another important feature in their home life that contributes to its success. The door is always open to clients who want their photographs taken and to friends who want to be fed. Gina and Hjalmar have created around them their own extended family.

Such is the marriage in which Gregers intervenes. It has obvious faults and imperfections, but the politics of family life in the Ekdal home are sufficiently balanced and harmonious to provide mutual society, help and comfort, which has been traditionally regarded as one of the key purposes of marriage. In respect of Gina and Hjalmar, Gregers's intervention at the end of Act 3 produces comic results, largely because of the discrepancy between his expectations of Hjalmar and the kind of man Hjalmar is in reality. Much of the laughter in Acts 4 and 5 is provoked by Hjalmar's sudden and erratic shifts of response, trapped as he is between Gina and Gregers. Gina's tactics in these two acts are to get Hjalmar sitting down at her table with some food in front of him. Inevitably, Gregers interrupts at the wrong moment, obliging Hjalmar to rise from Gina's table and act out the role of noble idealist that Gregers expects of him. At several moments, when Hjalmar is torn between sitting and standing, between the claims of the belly and the claims of the ideal, the action on stage borders on pure farce. Meanwhile, Gregers appears in an increasingly comic light as his misinterpretations of his friend's potential become progressively more grotesque.

However, Gregers's intervention also affects Hedvig. And here the element of tragedy running through the play stands out all the more clearly for being juxtaposed with Hjalmar's and Gina's comic responses. Hedvig is a child who knows no bitterness or hate in her responses to others, and her love for her parents is without reservation. She is receptive to Gregers's ideas because intuitively she feels his longing for authenticity. In Act 4, Gregers sows in her mind the thought of sacrificing the wild duck as the means of regaining her father's seemingly lost affection. Hjalmar's rejection of her is histrionic and immature. But Gregers's intervention in her life is worse: it is an act of violence clothed in the language of love, and it produces disastrous consequences. In her desperation, Hedvig comes to associate herself entirely with the wild duck and eventually shoots herself to prove her love for Hjalmar. She dies an innocent, even a spotless victim. What is left after her death is the memory of her grace, her unswerving love and commitment to those nearest her, her quiet and untutored dignity. Juxtaposed with the comic inadequacies of the other characters, the memory of these qualities gives the play its tragic stature.

Visually, *The Wild Duck* ends on a chaotically disintegrating note. While Hedvig's body is carried from the loft to her room downstage, Hjalmar indulges in comically incongruous rhetoric and shakes his fist at God. Gina is quiet and dignified. Old Ekdal, in full dress uniform, enters the loft to face up to the revenge of the forests. Molvik staggers out drunk. Meanwhile, Gregers and Relling quarrel bitterly and Gregers leaves with thoughts of suicide on his mind. Laughter and seriousness mix almost disconcertingly, but underneath the laughter here as elsewhere in the play the thrust of the action remains consistently serious. Ibsen's concern in analysing the politics of family life in *The Wild Duck* is to show the catastrophic effect of emotional violence, and particularly emotional violence masquerading as love. The confusion produced in Hedvig's case leads to her suicide; the confusion experienced by Gregers as a child has made him lethal as an adult in his dealings with others.

After this tragi-comic exploration of the politics of family life, Ibsen turned his attention in his next symbolist plays to an exploration of the politics of love. In both *Rosmersholm* and *Little Eyolf*, erotic fantasies blossom into strange and exotic shapes, as the major characters struggle to find a means of achieving sexual and emotional fulfilment across barriers erected by convention, guilt and memories of past experiences and relationships.

'Rosmersholm'

In *Rosmersholm*, the protagonists John Rosmer and Rebecca West act out a drama of thwarted romantic passion within a tightly controlled structural framework. Ibsen establishes a quite deliberate irony between the romantic texture of the action and the ordered restraint of the structure. With symmetrical precision, Acts 1 and 2 concentrate on John Rosmer, exploring his relationship with his late wife Beate and the way his feelings have developed since her suicide in the millrace. Acts 3 and 4 concentrate on Rebecca West, revealing the secrets of her past life with her adoptive father Dr West and her motives in coming to Rosmersholm. In a way that is reminiscent of *Ghosts*, the action of the past predominates over the action of the present, as the inner motivation and responses of the characters are laid bare. In the first three acts, outside interventions by Dr Kroll (a local headmaster and Beate's brother) and Mortensgård (a newspaper editor) spark off the process of mutual probing and analysis, including Rebecca's confession in Act 3 that she encouraged Beate to commit suicide. In the final act, it is Rosmer's return from town that provokes Rebecca into revealing her most closely guarded secret about the nature of her love for Rosmer. The effect produced by this structural pattern is to give Rosmer and Rebecca something of the stature of stylised lovers from neo-classic drama. Underneath all the neo-classic symmetry, however, the hero and heroine act out a late romantic drama of a passion so deadly it drives them both into the millrace.

Rosmersholm is set in a country manor house in Western Norway. The style of furnishing is typically *empire* in such houses, with generously proportioned chaises longues, sculptured chairs and an elegantly conceived décor. From Ibsen's description of the room, he seems to be envisaging something akin to a Baroque *scène à relief* in the way an upstage vista showing 'an avenue of tall old trees' can be glimpsed firstly through double doors leading to the hall and secondly through the outer door itself. Here, as in the structure of the play, one can detect a strong influence from the neo-classic theatre with its use of symmetrically patterned stage space, its *trompe l'oeil* and perspective painting. The same symmetry can be detected in Ibsen's suggestions for the placing of the furniture. A flower stand stage right counterbalances the wild flowers and birch branches decorating the stove stage left: a group of furniture stage left is juxtaposed with Rebecca's chair stage right. Within the symmetry, however, there is tension. Rebecca's large white shawl that she is crocheting and the profusion of fresh wild flowers and birch branches she has placed in the room are at odds with the formal elegance of the furnishing and the family portraits. Kroll draws attention to the fact as soon as he enters: 'Well, how pretty you've made this old room, flowers everywhere'.

As the action progresses, the lighting changes from soft evening twilight in Act 1, to the harsh morning sunlight of Acts 2 and 3 when a number of important discoveries and confessions are made. Finally, Act 4 takes place at night, in the eerie half-light of a summer night in the North, a lighting state well suited to the vibrant romanticism of this last act. The lamp is lit, but what makes the most important visual impact in the set is Rebecca's white shawl, draped over the downstage sofa. Rebecca's shawl, like her destiny, is completed: what now awaits her is death. For this her shawl will serve as the shroud in which she will wrap herself. It will also act as a visual reminder of the white horse of Rosmersholm that appears whenever someone is to die. By the end of the play, romantic images and symbols predominate visually within the neo-classic symmetry of the set, echoing and reinforcing what happens in the action of the play.

The central concern of *Rosmersholm* is the interaction of Rosmer and Rebecca. Both are complex individuals and their relationship is uneasy, tense, unbalanced by feelings of guilt. Rebecca is a decisive, even ruthless woman who once exploited and manipulated the emotions both of Kroll and of Beate to gain access to Rosmersholm and to be near Rosmer. We learn in Act 3 how she persuaded Beate to make way for her as her passion for Rosmer grew. We also learn in the same act how earlier in her life, after the death of her mother, she had assumed her mother's role as mistress in the house of her stepfather, Dr West. Guilty fantasies were built into the very fabric of that relationship. And Kroll makes it clear in Act 3 that those fantasies had some substance. Dr West was probably her real father, which means that Rebecca had for years committed incest. At Rosmersholm, as Freud pointed out in an essay on the play,[1] she has repeated the same pattern, involving herself in yet another guilt-inducing relationship with a father figure, Rosmer, after the suicide of a substitute mother figure, Beate, who was mistress of the house.

Rosmer, we learn in Act 2, played his part in Beate's unhappy end by refusing to meet her need for emotional and sexual warmth. His revulsion at what he called her 'wild uncontrolled passion that she longed for me to reciprocate', had the effect of convincing Beate that she was both sick and mad and had no right to be Rosmer's wife. So she made way. Since then Rosmer has lived out a fantasy of platonic friendship with Rebecca, retiring early to his study every night, hoping for restful nights undisturbed by wild dreams and carefully avoiding the bridge over the millrace from where Beate leapt to her death.

Neither Rosmer nor Rebecca find it easy to throw Beate's corpse off their back (as Rosmer expresses it in Act 2). Instead the memory of Beate seems to exercise an increasingly powerful hold over them. As the play progresses, both of them become preoccupied with thoughts of death. The Death Horn, as Gordon Craig called it in a note on his 1906 production of the play, sounds with growing frequency in the dialogue. At the end of Act 3, there are extended references to the main symbol of death in the play, the White Horse of Rosmersholm. At the beginning of Act 4, Rebecca's white shawl serves as a visual reminder of the White Horse. Later in Act 4, Ulrik Brendel, Rosmer's childhood tutor, spells out some of the murderous thoughts that are in the back of Rosmer's mind: 'Victory is assured. But – mark well – upon one unavoidable condition. [. . .] That the woman who loves him goes gladly into the kitchen and chops off her rosy little finger – here – just at the middle joint. Item. That the aforesaid loving woman – likewise gladly – snips off her incomparably moulded left ear.' Brendel not only articulates the kind of proof that Rosmer will demand of Rebecca, but in his choice of Freudian sexual images (finger and ear as symbols of male and female sexual organs) he also makes it clear that the need for Rebecca's death is inextricably linked in Rosmer's mind with the need for her to divest herself of her sexuality. Like a clown figure out of a play by Samuel Beckett, Brendel expresses what Rosmer and Rebecca hardly dare think. After his exit, however, they both begin to articulate their hidden thoughts.

Rebecca claims that her former passion for Rosmer has subsided into a gentle tender emotion, free from any taint of sexuality. Rosmer spells out the proof he wants of her new-found love for him: 'Have you the courage to – are you willing to – gladly as Ulrik Brendel said – for my sake, now, tonight – gladly – to go the same way – as Beate went?' Like a tongue-tied youth, Rosmer sits on the edge of his seat stumbling over every word. The note of erotic arousal is unmistakable. He admits that there is 'a horrible fascination' in his thoughts, but almost in the same breath recoils from the prospect opened up in his mind: 'All this. It's sheer madness'. And the sense of erotic madness is heightened for Rosmer by the knowledge that what he has in mind is not making love to a young woman but using her corpse, or rather the thought of her corpse, as a vehicle for erotic satisfaction.

Rebecca not only catches Rosmer's mood, sharing his sense of anticipation and excitement, she seems to know what is in his mind almost before he shapes his thoughts into words: 'Yes, John, say it and you shall see'. Now that Rosmer offers her his trust and love on the only terms he can, Rebecca finds it impossible to deny him. She willingly allows Rosmer to determine the nature and shape of their relationship. Even when this means her death, she gladly assents: 'You shall have your faith again. [. . .] You must judge in the morning – or later, when they fetch me up'.

In his analysis of the politics of love in *Rosmersholm*, Ibsen shows his protagonists pursuing changing strategies of dominance and submission. To begin with, Rebecca plays the dominant role in their relationship and imposes on Rosmer a liberated image that is completely at odds with his conservative instincts. Rebecca admits in Act 3 that she acted decisively to free Rosmer from his unhappy marriage and then steered him away from his political conservatism towards the idealism of the Radicals. During the action of the play, she discovers that all her strategies have failed. Rosmer's basic emotional and political instincts have remained unchanged. Instead of moulding her lover into a liberated individual, she has merely burdened him with a crippling legacy of guilt. In Act 4, the positions are reversed. As Rebecca finds herself 'infected' by Rosmer's feelings of guilt, Rosmer assumes the dominant role in their relationship and imposes on her his idiosyncratic view of life – a strange mixture of emotional and sexual immaturity, coupled with an Old Testament moral conservatism. By the end of Act 4, Rebecca is refashioned into a submissive partner who denies her sexual feelings and who claims that she must now atone for her sins. The one thing they both fail to achieve is a relaxed acceptance of each other as they actually are. Their various attempts to coerce each other into submissive behaviour are shown to be acts of emotional violence.

In the end, they go together. And there is a poignant sense of loss and waste in their death. There is also great ambiguity in the motives that ultimately prompt their suicide. They claim to be expiating past sins by dying. Memories of falsehood, incest and murder in Rebecca's case: emotional cruelty, complicity in murder and even necrophiliac fantasies in Rosmer's case. Viewed in this light, their death reaffirms the moral law that was transgressed when Beate was driven to suicide. But at the same time, their death is prompted by an irresistible erotic drive, barely articulated but nevertheless acknowledged in Rosmer's symbolic wedding ceremony with Rebecca: 'Now I lay my hand on your head and take you in marriage to be my truly wedded wife'. The carefully preserved decorum of the ending, with its neo-classic understatement, points to the triumph of order and morality. But what is acted out, underneath the dialogue and within the precise symmetry of structure and setting, is a vibrantly romantic drama of love and passion in which the protagonists succumb to the lure of erotically destructive fantasy. As Rosmer and Rebecca exit to celebrate their strange love feast in the millrace, Ibsen invites his audience to feel an emotional sympathy for them in their dilemma and at the same time to stand back and judge them dispassionately.

'Little Eyolf'

In his next play exploring the politics of love, *Little Eyolf*, the invitation to stand back and judge the behaviour of the characters is even more clearly built into the fabric of the work. Alfred Allmers leads the life of a gentleman scholar, having married a beautiful and wealthy landowner, Rita, for the sake of her 'gold and green forests'. Whatever affection he may once have felt for his wife has long since faded. His emotional life is now dominated by incestuous fantasies involving his half-sister Asta. Unwilling or unable

117

to acknowledge the reality of what he feels, Alfred leads a life of emotional self-deception. The action of the play traces the effects of this on his wife, on his son little Eyolf, and on Asta.

Structurally, the play follows a simple three-act pattern, in which Act 1 is built around a forward-moving action that introduces the different characters and the hidden tensions in their relationships; Act 2 is predominantly retrospective in nature, exploring the past relationships between Alfred and the two women in his life, Asta and Rita; in Act 3 the action is exclusively forward-moving, bringing to a head the crisis in the lives of Alfred, Asta and Rita and showing how the crisis is resolved. Within this simple structural framework, Ibsen employs a series of verbal and visual symbols (including a number of verbal leitmotivs) to add depth and resonance to the action and, even more importantly, to fuse together the worlds of conscious and subconscious experience.

Act 1 is dominated by the mysterious symbolic figure of the Rat Wife with her dog Mopseman. In terms of the overt action, the Rat Wife lures Eyolf to his death by drowning at the end of the act. But Ibsen also uses her (like Brendel in *Rosmersholm*) as a means of articulating hidden thoughts in the minds of the main characters, Rita and Alfred. Rita resents the way her son Eyolf acts as a barrier between herself and her husband. Secretly she wishes him out of the way, just like the Rat Wife's clients who employ her to entice the rats from their homes. The Rat Wife underlines the parallel by showing her dog to Eyolf, the dog that both he and the rats find ugly and yet irresistibly lovely. Alfred is so torn by guilt (he feels guilty for marrying Rita, guilty for leaving Asta to get married, guilty because his son was crippled as a child through his negligence) that he longs for the peace and solitude of death in the high mountains, just as the Rat Wife describes the rats longing for the calm of death when she entices them into the fjord.

An important visual and verbal image throughout Act 1 is Eyolf's crutch. It serves as a reminder to Alfred that he once succumbed to Rita's 'devastating' beauty and made love to her when he should have been watching his child asleep on a table. Eyolf fell and was crippled as a result. Alfred experiences the sight of the crutch as a constant reproach; it encapsulates all his feelings of guilt. Rita's feelings of guilt only begin after Eyolf's death. She expresses them with the verbal image of Eyolf's crutch described as floating on the water. All she ever wanted was a fulfilled and complete relationship with Alfred. But that he has always denied her. Since Eyolf's fall, he has used the child as an excuse to avoid close contact with her. The emotional and sexual frustration this has produced in Rita has driven her to think evil thoughts. She wanted Eyolf out of the way in order to come closer to her husband. Now that Eyolf is dead, she finds that she and Alfred are stricken with the kind of remorse that drives them even further apart. Eyolf still stands between them, as she herself says: 'Now perhaps more than ever' [viii, p. 78].

A number of important verbal images recur during the action. Rita's 'gold and green forests' is used in Acts 1 and 2 to sum up her physical and material wealth that Alfred has merely exploited. Alfred married her for her material wealth, but her physical beauty and sensual warmth terrify him. He is willing to live off her parasitically, but not genuinely with her, accepting her for what she is. As Rita expresses it in Act 1, with her mind and body she offered him champagne, but he 'touched it not'.

'The law of change' is a leitmotiv that recurs during Acts 2 and 3. Alfred cannot come to terms with the fact that the whole of life is subject to 'the law of change'. The repeated

119

reference to this notion underlines his folly in wishing to cling fast to a fantasy relationship with Asta at a particular frozen moment of time. More than ten years ago, when they lived together as orphans and she was still a young girl, she dressed in boys' clothes; Alfred called her Eyolf and allowed her to be for him sister, brother and little mother in a complex sexual fantasy. But Asta is now a grown woman who has discovered that she is not after all Alfred's half-sister. (Asta's mother, it seems, had an affair and was made pregnant by her lover.) Alfred refuses to acknowledge that life has moved on, subject to the law of change. Asta can only resolve the untenable nature of their relationship by fleeing with Borghejm, the roadbuilder.

After Asta's departure in Act 3 Alfred is obsessed with the lure of death, expressed in his longing for the solitude of the high mountains. Even when he agrees to stay with Rita so that they can both devote themselves to good works by educating the poor children of the town, it is still towards the mountains, the stars, and the vast silence of death that he looks.

Visually, the play moves from an elegant and richly appointed interior in Act 1 that expresses the warmth and voluptuousness of Rita's personality to contrasting outdoor settings in Acts 2 and 3. Act 2 is set by the side of the fjord, with the characters enveloped in a driving mist as they wrestle with their grief and guilt-ridden memories of the past. Act 3 is set at a high point in the garden on a clear summer evening, as the major characters face up to the crisis confronting them and resolve it. At the end of the play, the flag flying at half-mast to mark Eyolf's death is fully raised by Alfred, confirming symbolically his new-found sense of purpose.

In terms of movement and blocking, the play is centred on Alfred. He is constantly on stage, apart from brief scenes at the opening of Acts 1 and 3. Even then, the other characters on stage are preoccupied with him in their thoughts. The action revolves quite literally around him, as Asta and Rita seek him out and respond to his every whim. Alfred's primary emotional need is for Asta. The social taboo against incest has so far prevented him from sleeping with her. But this only multiplies the fantasy images that fill his mind. His one aim in life is to keep her near him. It was for Asta's sake that he married a wealthy partner. That at least guaranteed them a measure of economic indepen- dence. But now he wants her preserved for ever as his little half-sister, dressed in boys' clothing, seeing to his every need. His relationship with her is exploitative. He cannot accept the fact that she is now a grown woman with her own life to lead. In Act 3, even after he has learnt that she is not his half-sister, he still attempts to impose on her the fantasy image to which he clings: 'Stay. And share your life with us, Asta. With Rita. With me. With me – your brother' [viii, p. 96]. No wonder Asta flees from him and throws herself into the arms of another man as the only means of preserving her self-respect and her sanity.

Alfred's relationship with Rita is based on deliberate exploitation. He married her for entirely selfish reasons. Ever since, he has found a series of excuses to avoid her. First his book on 'human responsibility', then Eyolf's education, finally Eyolf's death. He has also instinctively attempted to make Rita feel guilty for being the warm and sensuous person she is. According to Alfred, it was her beauty that was to blame for Eyolf's fall. In addition, by claiming that her emotional and sexual needs terrified him, he implies that they were abnormal. Consistently, he subjects his wife to a pattern of remorseless emotional violence. Unlike Beate, Rita is strong and defiant enough to retain her sanity, but she finds herself driven by Alfred's tactics into thinking evil and destructive thoughts as the potential for love withers within her.

The politics of love acted out in their relationship involve Alfred in a constant search for new ways of forcing Rita into a docile, submissive role, where she will make no sexual demands of him. By the end of the play, he succeeds almost entirely in his aim. Rita makes a bid for dominant status at the end of Act 3 when she asserts her determination to devote herself to social good works if Alfred leaves her. Alfred's response is to annexe her vision (he would never have thought of helping the poor, despite his book on human responsibility) and emasculate it by confusing it with his self-indulgent romanticising on death. Rita accepts his travesty of her vision as long as it involves a life shared with him. She confirms her willingness to accept a submissive, undemanding role by 'thanking' him as he directs their gaze towards the mountains, the stars, the vast silence.

The quite deliberate irony of this ending underlines just how dangerous Alfred can be in his interaction with others. His strategies succeed in reducing a warm-blooded woman like Rita to a shadow of herself who 'thanks' him for channelling her thoughts towards the icy calm of death. Meanwhile, Asta has fled from his violence to a man who will offer her genuine warmth and affection. As in *Rosmersholm*, we see that the politics of love can have lethal consequences. But at least Asta escapes. The fate of Rebecca West, who just failed to escape from Rosmersholm, helps to explain why Asta flees so precipitately from both Alfred and herself. At the end of the play, Alfred and Rita take refuge from the pain of real experience in a fantasy scenario of social good works, sustained by the hope of glimpsing in their minds from time to time those they have lost: as Rita expresses it, 'Our little Eyolf. And your big Eyolf too'. But as they direct their gaze upwards, the only reality they acknowledge is the vast silence of death.

'The Master Builder'

Ibsen's two remaining symbolist plays, *The Master Builder* and *When we dead awaken*, touch on love themes already explored in *Little Eyolf* and *Rosmersholm*. But they are both predominantly concerned with analysing the politics of art and creativity. At the very end of his career as a dramatist, Ibsen returns to a theme that had preoccupied him in his early years as a poet and playwright, namely the role of the artist and the clash between art and life. Both plays are strongly autobiographical and amount to a searing reckoning with his own life, as Ibsen shows the artist figures Solness and Rubek ruthlessly manipulating and exploiting the people who are closest to them. Their exploitation extends beyond the normal limits of interaction into the very thoughts, dreams and subconscious wishes of their victims.

In *The Master Builder*, the whole action revolves around Solness in a manner that is reminiscent of an expressionist dream play. For instance, Solness only has to voice his fear of youth knocking at the door in Act 1, when at once Hilde Wangel knocks at the door and enters his life. Characters and events are as if conjured up out of his fantasy. In visual and structural terms, he is the constant focus of attention. There is very little forward-moving action in the play, and most of this is confined to the very beginning and the very end. The remainder of the three acts is given over in part to a retrospective exploration of Solness's life, and in part to a series of extended dream-like scenes between Solness and Hilde where they build 'castles in the air'.

The event that sparks off the action is the request by an

employee of the master builder, Ragnar Brovik, that he should be allowed to submit his own designs for one of Solness's clients. This event crystallises for Solness his fears of young rivals who will challenge his pre-eminence and eventually sweep him aside. The remainder of the action explores in detail his fears of failing creative and sexual potency. He is intent on keeping youth down, but is eventually destroyed by his arrogant determination to remain on top. Retribution comes, as he always feared, through youth. Hilde Wangel appears in the action, like a figment of his imagination, to drive him onwards and upwards to the point where he fails and falls to his death from a tower he himself has built but cannot climb.

The play revolves around images of potency and impotence. From the outset, a strong link is established between sexual and creative potency. Creativity points to the sky like a tower. Solness's creativity, like his sexual potency, is in doubt. In Act 1, he still has enough power to make his secretary, Kaja Fosli, tremble just by looking at her behind her back. He also runs his office with a rod of steel, ruthlessly exploiting the skills of his subordinates, while destroying their faith in themselves to ensure that they never seek to rival him. However, when Hilde Wangel appears towards the end of Act 1, Solness's potency is put to the test.

She first saw him (we learn in Act 1) as a young child some ten years previously when he built a church tower at Lysanger. His climb right up the tower to place the builder's wreath on the very top has always associated him in her mind with images of phallic potency. According to her, he met her that evening, bent her back and kissed her many times. He also promised her a kingdom in ten years' time. Hilde has now come to claim her kingdom and is delighted to discover at the very end of Act 1 that Solness has actually built another tower, this time on his new home. By the end of Act 2, Hilde urges Solness to climb his own tower at the topping-out ceremony.

In Act 3, they dream together of castles in the air, with high towers that the master builder will have to climb if he wants to visit his princess. At the end of the act, he attempts just that, climbing the tower on his new house at the topping-out ceremony in order to please his princess. But Solness's powers are already failing; he cannot in reality climb as high as he builds. While Hilde shouts and waves encouragement to him, he falls from the tower and is killed.

A number of resonant images are used during the play to explore the nature of Solness's artistry. Notably in Act 2, when he tells Hilde of the events that led to his success, including the burning down of his wife's house, he sees himself in vivid terms as a man almost possessed, almost mad, who can call on hidden helpers and servants. It is as if, like Faust, he has made a pact with the Devil. Certainly he sees God as an adversary ever since he wrestled with Him on top of the tower at Lysanger and resolved to build no more churches but homes for people. But the price he has had to pay for his artistry, for being able to call on his helpers and servers, is a high one and has involved renouncing any personal happiness. Also those closest to him have had to suffer. Solness sums up what this means in a striking image towards the end of Act 2: 'It feels as if my breast were a great expanse of raw flesh. And these helpers and servants go flaying off the skin from other people's bodies to patch *my* wound. Yet the wound never heals . . . never!' [vii, p. 412]. Creativity, as he experiences it, is not a gift but a searing pain that can never be stilled.

Solness's wife, Aline, introduces yet another set of resonant images into the action. She has suffered most from Solness's ruthlessness, and life for her as a result is a living death. Solness had longed for his wife's family home to burn down and release valuable building land. When it did, his career was assured. While Solness prospered, Aline's life was filled with a sense of emptiness and loss. The fire that launched Solness contributed to the death of Aline's twin babies and destroyed all the possessions that established for her a sense of family and identity, including dresses and jewellery and nine beautiful dolls. When she is talking to Hilde at the beginning of Act 3, it almost seems as if Aline regretted the loss of her dolls more than her babies. Drained of any vitality, she is now a hollow shell of a woman for whom life is no more than a series of meaningless duties and obligations. Hilde tells Solness in Act 3 that talking to Aline is like being locked in a tomb with the frost seizing one's bones. Aline is always dressed in black. At the end of the play, she wears a white shawl, a symbolic shroud that Hilde snatches and waves when Solness climbs to the top of his tower. Its effect is deadly.

The imagery associated with Hilde is vivacious and throbbing with life. When she first appears, she is in walking gear, with a long alpenstock, a rucksack and her skirts hitched up for hiking. She likens herself in Act 2 to a bird of prey, with something of the troll inside her. Her use of the stage space is inquisitive and impetuous, like that of a child, and her expressions of delight are quite spontaneous. In Act 2, for instance, she shows her gratitude to Aline by throwing her arms around her neck, which causes Aline considerable embarrassment. In Act 3, the contrast between them is further underlined in visual terms when Aline is wrapped in a large white shawl whereas Hilde has a little bunch of small garden flowers pinned to her breast. Significantly, however, Hilde snatches Aline's shroud-like shawl to wave Solness on to his doom at the end of the act.

The stage setting is used to underline important aspects

of characterisation and mood. The lay-out in Act 1 demonstrates visually Solness's hold over the various characters working for him. Kaja Fosli stands downstage at her desk, which allows Solness to dominate her from behind: while he can observe and exploit her every movement, she is bound to her desk and her work, trembling at the thought of his gaze. Her fiancé Ragnar Brovik and Brovik's father both slave away in an upstage office. Only in Solness's absence do they freely dare to leave their confined area of work. When Solness is present, any encroachment they make into the downstage area is cautious and deferential. Act 2 is set in Aline's domain, a small sitting-room with an almost oppressive profusion of plants. It is as if Aline has filled her house with plants to make up for her lost children and to compensate for the emptiness in the three nurseries the house possesses. Against this visual background, Solness confesses to Hilde his feelings of guilt towards his wife. The thriving plants and flowers add substance to his claim that Aline had a vocation in life that was crushed, 'a talent for building children's souls'. Act 3 is dominated by images associated with Hilde. The setting is a verandah looking on to Solness's garden. Hilde's link with the garden is stressed by the little bunch of garden flowers she wears; Aline even draws attention to the fact in the dialogue. Right down to this last symbolic detail, Hilde is associated with fresh air and spontaneity. The upstage vista is dominated by the image of the tower on Solness's house. Hilde drives Solness towards the tower to prove his artistic and sexual potency, while Aline tries to dissuade him, and the young builders gather to laugh at his fear of heights.

The patterns of interaction in the play are quite different from anything Ibsen had previously attempted. In his analysis of the politics of art, Ibsen shows the artist manipulating and exploiting others at the subliminal level of dream and subconscious fantasy. Like Prospero, Solness can conjure up people, events, destinies. His artistic vision, as he describes it to Hilde in Act 3, was initially based on an idealistic commitment to build for the glory of God. After the death of his twin sons, his vision has become more prosaically humanistic, a commitment to build homes for people. Throughout his life, however, Solness has pursued his artistic vocation selfishly and arrogantly. During the action of the play, we watch him ruthlessly suppress young and old rivals; we see him in Act 1 use his charisma to subjugate the will of his secretary and helper, Kaja Fosli, until he brutally discards her when he no longer needs her; in Act 2 we observe his guilt-ridden responses to his wife whose life he has helped to drain of all vitality. His only excuse is to claim to Hilde that it was the troll or demon that forced him on. But as he looks back over the ruins of his life in Act 2, he is eaten up by guilt, paralysed by the knowledge of what he has done.

Consumed by a sense of failure and remorse, the master builder dreams up a figure who brings retribution: Hilde Wangel, the embodiment of youth, the youth that he fears but to which he is 'drawn so sorely'. In their scenes together, she manipulates him as ruthlessly as he has always exploited and used others. In her too there is a troll, a wild bird of prey that wants to get its claws into its victims. In the end she succeeds. Hilde represents the impossible, for which Solness has always longed. In reaching towards her across the boundaries of time, space, reality and dream, Solness attempts the impossible and dies.

Solness is a self-taught artist who has reached the top of his profession by dint of technical skill and personal charisma. But his art, like his life, is devoid of love. It is based, not on a loving acceptance of others, but on the violent exploitation of the needs and feelings of those closest to him. No wonder he describes it in Act 2 as a dear purchase: 'All this I somehow have to make up for. Pay for. Not in money. But in human happiness. And not with my own happiness alone. But also with others' ' [vii, p. 406]. In falling to his death, a victim of his own arrogant vision, Solness acts out a judgement on himself. It was not his pursuit of art that was wrong, but the ruthlessness of that pursuit. He dies, like the Emperor Julian, a shattered instrument of the Lord, a victim of the world will that cannot tolerate an imbalanced and distorted assertion of the ideal.

'When we dead awaken'

Much the same is true of Rubek in *When we dead awaken*. But there is more sense of reconciliation than in *The Master Builder*. Rubek, like Solness, has pursued his artistic vision at the expense of others. But in his case, he has more clearly sold out to the forces of materialism. Material greed and ambition have become a cancer, gnawing at the fabric of Rubek's creativity until he has become completely sterile, utterly devoid of inspiration. The action of the play traces his final reckoning with himself as he decisively rejects the material values and life-style of his middle years and reaffirms the purity of his original commitment.

When we dead awaken is a subtle and complex play that blends together the spheres of everyday reality and universal, mythical experience. The action begins at the level of lived-out reality, showing the way the four major characters in the play interact with each other: an ageing sculptor Rubek, his young wife Maja, his former model Irene and a hunter called Squire Ulfhejm. Gradually, these various characters are linked with figures from classical and

Christian mythology in a way that adds subtle resonances to their pattern of behaviour in the play.

The action follows a dream-like pattern, reminiscent of a late quartet by Beethoven or Schubert. Acts 1 and 2 open with forward-moving scenes in which Rubek and Maja discuss their dissatisfaction with each other and their decision to part. Both acts close with extended encounters between Rubek and Irene where the action is predominantly retrospective. Act 1 concentrates on exploring Irene's life after Rubek had rejected her. Act 2 delves into Rubek's life after Irene's departure. This mutual probing of the past prepares the ground for the final act in which Rubek and Irene climb to a triumphant *Liebestod* in the mountains while Maja descends to an earth-bound existence with Squire Ulfhejm.

The physical setting of the play clearly indicates the way the action progresses from reality to myth. Act 1 is set in the grounds of a hotel at a coastal spa town. The stage directions call for emblems of material prosperity and well-being. A couple seated in basket chairs sipping champagne and seltzer after breakfast. A gracious park with fountains, carefully planted shrubs, a small vine-clad pavilion and glimpses of a pleasing fjord landscape in the distance. The atmosphere is one of listless boredom, reflecting the state of Rubek's and Maja's marriage. Act 2 moves from the expensive ennui of this environment to an austerely challenging mountain landscape. The setting is a vast treeless plateau that stretches away towards a long mountain lake: beyond there is a range of snow-clad mountain peaks. The 'dead country', as Irene calls it, is a place where the protective masks and subterfuges of everyday reality can be stripped away. Act 3 moves to the mountain peaks, a landscape where myth is more important than reality. Architecturally structured stage space and swathes of light are envisaged in the stage directions, anticipating the techniques of the expressionist theatre. As Rubek and Irene climb through the mists to the mountain peaks at the end of the act, the visual imagery underlines their spiritual progress from self-delusion to self-transcendence.

The various mythical references in the play begin with the names of the two women, Irene and Maja, although it is only as the action progresses that the significance of these names becomes apparent. Irene, or Eirene in Greek mythology, takes her name from one of the three Horae, a goddess of the seasons, but also a goddess of fate. Eirene's function was to bring peace to mankind. Irene has a number of similarities with her namesake in Greek mythology. She loves beauty in art and nature and longs to be fruitful in her own life. She intervenes in Rubek's life like a goddess of fate, but with the aim, not of seeking revenge, but of bringing peace of mind to them both.

Maja takes her name from the goddess of earth and fertility. Appropriately, her attitude to life is earthy and spontaneous: her needs basic and material. She cannot understand Rubek's spiritual torments; all she wants from him is warmth and affection. When Maja discovers in Act 1 that Rubek has grown bored with her, she turns her attention to an earthy uncomplicated man, Squire Ulfhejm, who hunts anything that crosses his path. In Act 3 Ulfhejm tries to rape Maja, and she likens him to a faun, that strange beast from Greek mythology, half-man, half-goat. Ulfhejm confesses wryly that he has turned into a lecherous goat because he was jilted by a girl in his youth. Towards the end of Act 3, Maja and her faun establish an understanding that takes them back down to earth and to a relationship that, for all its imperfections, is nevertheless based on mutual warmth and support.

Rubek is not obviously linked by name with any specific mythical figure. But as the action progresses, a number of oblique associations are made that link him with figures from Christian mythology. In both Acts 1 and 2, a parallel is drawn between Rubek and the Devil. Using the same words as the Devil to Christ, Rubek promised both Maja and Irene to take them up a high mountain and show them all the glory of the world, provided they would fall down and worship him. Rubek's promises proved to be as empty as the Devil's. But the hubris of which he is guilty in even making such a claim indicates how tainted and corrupt his life has become.

In Act 2, when he and Irene throw leaves and petals into a mountain stream, Irene recalls the occasion when they first played that particular game on the banks of the Taunitzer See. The water-lilies and dock leaves they threw into the waters of the lake became 'Lohengrin's boat with the swan drawing it'. Rubek as a young artist saw himself in the role of Lohengrin as a servant of the Holy Grail of art, dedicated to a life of chastity, self-sacrifice and service. Irene was his swan, drawing him on like Lohengrin to meet the challenges of art. Since then his vision has been marred by worldly ambition and success. In Act 3, however, Irene, dressed in her swansdown hood, once again takes up her role vis-à-vis Rubek as Lohengrin, drawing him on to a deeper understanding of art and human life. Fleetingly and evocatively, these various images extend the action of the play into the sphere of mythical experience, preparing the way for the decisive shift from reality to myth during Act 3.[2]

The central concern in *When we dead awaken* is the relationship between Rubek and Irene. As they probe the past together in Acts 1 and 2, we learn that Irene had been Rubek's model years ago, but had left him when he hinted insultingly that he no longer needed her. He had used her, body and soul, for his masterpiece 'The Day of Resurrection'. Sharing the same purity of vision as Rubek, Irene had sacrificed herself willingly. But after he had discarded her, Irene could no longer see herself as a chaste partner who had collaborated with Rubek in the task of expressing an inner purity of vision. She was simply a woman whose body and soul had been ruthlessly exploited. The result of this decisive experience was a disaster for both of them.

Irene deliberately degraded herself, first as a stripper, then in a series of money-based marriages. She drove several wealthy but stupid husbands to distraction until she herself broke under the strain and ended up in the padded cell of a lunatic asylum. Rubek meanwhile became a prisoner of his vaulting ambition and surrounded himself with all the marks of worldly success. He married a pretty young wife, bought expensive property and travelled widely. As an artist, he was content to be a purveyor of artistic consumer goods to wealthy clients and even altered his masterpiece to bring it more in line with his new materialistic outlook. Looking back on their respective lives at the end of Act 2, Irene comments: 'We only see what we have missed when [. . .] we dead awaken. [. . .] We see that we have never lived' [viii, pp. 285–6].

It is not until Act 3 that Rubek finally rejects the materialism that has destroyed his creativity. Amidst the mountain peaks, with the wind rising and an avalanche threatening, Rubek finally accepts the validity of Irene's view of their lives. And in so doing, he accepts her for what she is, his bride of grace. No longer does he attempt to impose any kind of role on her. Instead, he climbs with her to share a love feast, 'in the glory and the splendour of the light'. For the first time in his life, he gives himself completely and unselfishly to another. It is too late for Rubek and Irene to relive their lives, but not too late for them to make their death a triumphant assertion of their shared commitment to each other and to the purity of vision that once inspired them both.

Despite the dark tonality of the play, Ibsen's final reckoning with himself and with the politics of art concludes on a note of life-affirming reconciliation. The closing words of the play, 'Pax vobiscum', taken from the end of the late nineteenth-century Lutheran mass, indicate that Irene and Rubek have progressed from a state of sin and confusion, through mutual confession and understanding, to a state of grace. This final benediction, spoken by a sister of mercy, completes the action of a play in which the worlds of lived-out relationships, myth and even liturgy are carefully and evocatively woven together.

In his various social plays, Ibsen's aim had been to explore, as he himself said, 'human beings, human moods and human destinies, seen against a background of contemporary social conditions and attitudes'. In his symbolist plays, there was a subtle shift of emphasis from the social to the personal. His stated aim in *Rosmersholm*, for instance, was to write, 'a poem about human beings and human destinies'.[3] What this meant in practical terms was an intense and detailed exploration of human relationships, using visual and verbal imagery to add complex resonances to that exploration, in order to penetrate through the surface skin of reality and expose the deeper, hidden patterns underneath. Each of his symbolist plays was, in T. S. Eliot's words, 'a raid on the inarticulate'.

A consistent theme emerges from his symbolist plays in the juxtaposition of love and violence. Different facets of human interaction are explored in each play, but a recurring pattern can be perceived in the way characters, in the name of 'love' or 'art' or 'the claims of the ideal', subject others to extreme emotional violence in order to dominate them and force them into submissive behaviour. A similar technique is used in Pinter's plays as characters wrestle with each other for dominant status in terms of territory or possessions or hierarchy. But where Pinter simply shows these hidden, subtextual patterns and invites his audience to accept them as a bleak and sardonic demonstration of man's predatory instincts, Ibsen, in complete contrast, invites a clear judgement on those characters who subject others to destructive and devastating pressure.

Ibsen's work is sustained by a passionate commitment to a vision of unselfish love that is either implied or stated in all his plays. (And his vision is strikingly similar to that of Paul in 1 Corinthians 13, where love is defined as 'patient', 'kind', 'never selfish', with 'no limit to its faith, its hope, and its endurance'.) This vision acts as a yardstick against which we are invited to judge the behaviour and responses of his various characters: the lethal self-absorption of Rosmer, Solness and Allmers; the instinctive warmth and grace of Hedvig contrasted with the coldness and hatred in Gregers's soul; Irene's unselfish love and commitment contrasted with Rubek's greed and ambition. In certain plays, the audience is invited implicitly to supply the positive vision that has eluded the major characters. But in others, it is explicitly stated and embodied in the words and deeds of one or more characters. Ibsen was firmly committed to the notion that human beings create for themselves significance or absurdity through the nature and quality of their interaction with each other. By tracing, in minute detail, how his characters both create and destroy meaning for each other in the way they relate to each other, Ibsen offers us in his symbolist plays a lasting and timeless insight into the politics and poetry of human lives and human destinies. Few playwrights have since matched the quality and complexity of that insight.

6
Ibsen in Production

After his break with the theatre in the early 1860s, Ibsen rarely went to see any of his plays in production. He did, however, take a lively interest in the casting and staging of his plays in Christiania and was particularly keen that his work should be performed regularly by Scandinavia's most prestigious theatre, The Theatre Royal in Copenhagen. His letters to the Christiania Theatre contain a number of revealing insights into the way he envisaged a particular role being played and into the overall tone, pace and mood he wanted the actors to achieve in production. A few representative examples must suffice here.[1]

In respect of *Pillars of Society*, he wrote as follows on 21 November 1878:

> Permit me to suggest that the pace throughout, and particularly in the most emotive scenes, should be faster than is normally the case at the Christiania Theatre. I also hope that appropriate attention will be paid to the grouping and placing of the characters. Any tendency for

137

the actors to congregate downstage should be avoided, and their relative positions on stage should change whenever it seems natural; generally, every scene and every visual image should be, as far as possible, a reflection of reality. Thoughtless actors might be tempted to caricature some of the characters in the play. I hope this won't happen; I want complete truth to life in every respect.

Ibsen had experienced at first hand the neo-classic and romantic traditions of the Norwegian theatre. Although a play like *Pillars of Society* drew on these traditions, with its use of visually attractive tableaux, it nevertheless demanded a completely new style of realistic acting and directing. Ibsen stresses here that the overall effect he wants to create on stage is a natural reflection of everyday reality. This means that moves, gestures and blocking need to flow organically from the interaction of the characters on stage, instead of being a reflection of routine-based conventions in which actors relied on individual mannerisms and stock gestures to appeal to their audiences. He specifically warns against the traditional grouping of actors in a downstage position around the prompter's box. It is also interesting to note that, in terms of acting style, he wants the comic qualities in the play to be brought out through an overall fast pace rather than through any hint of caricature or parody.

In discussing a possible cast for *The Wild Duck*, Ibsen had the following points to make in November 1884 about the part of Hjalmar Edkal:

Hjalmar must not be acted with any trace of parody. The actor must at no point show that he is conscious that there is anything funny in what he says. His voice has, as

Relling observes, something endearing about it, and this
quality must be clearly brought out. His sentimentality is
honest, his melancholy, in its way, attractive; no hint of
affectation. Between ourselves, I would suggest you cast
your mind towards Kristofer Jansen, who still strives to
create an effect of beauty whatever nonsense he may be
uttering. There is a pointer for whoever plays the part.
[. . .] The play demands absolute naturalness and truth-
fulness both in the ensemble work and in the staging.

Once again, Ibsen stresses the importance of a natural, true
to life approach in terms of staging and acting. This time,
however, he explains his opposition to any trace of parody
in the acting. What he wants from the actors is for them to
view their parts sympathetically from within, allowing the
audience to note the comic incongruity of the characters'
responses. This marks a complete break with the traditional satiric approach of actors in neo-classic comedy (by,
for instance, Molière or Holberg) who guide and channel
the audience's response by exaggerating the failings of a
given character to the point of parody. The emotional
identification Ibsen expects from his actors explains the
importance he attached to casting.

The same point emerges from his comments on a
planned production of *Rosmersholm* in January 1887:

You feel that Mrs Gundersen is an obvious choice to play
'Rebecca'. This is not the case. Mrs Gundersen's strength
lies in declaiming grand, rhetorical dialogue; and there
isn't any in my play. How would she cope with dialogue
that seems light but has hidden depths? And anyway,
complex characters with split personalities are simply not
her strong point. And then you want Gundersen to play
'Rosmer'. Permit me to enquire what it will look like

when Rebecca explains that she was gripped by a 'wild, sensual desire' for him. Or when Brendel calls him 'my boy'. Or when Kroll imposes on him and dominates him. Is Gundersen's character in any way compatible with this and much more? For Rosmer you must choose the most delicate and refined personality the theatre possesses.

Here Ibsen makes it quite clear that the established rhetorical conventions of Romantic acting would be completely inappropriate as a means of portraying the subtle and elusive characters in his play. He leaves the theatre manager in no doubt that he wants actors who have a physical and spiritual affinity with the characters they are to portray. Instead of an externalised, rhetorical approach to acting, what he envisaged was an acting style based on emotional empathy.

These various notes presuppose a detailed naturalism in terms of acting and directing that was very different in quality from the rhetorical, routine-based theatre Ibsen had known in his youth. Naturalist approaches to directing were being tried in Germany and Scandinavia at the time, but a naturalist theatre style was not fully developed until the late 1880s. Even though he had broken off direct physical contact with the theatre, it is apparent from these letters that Ibsen was in the vanguard of theatrical thinking at the time. Zola, for instance, in his book *Naturalism in the Theatre* (1881), wanted to see theatrical conventions altered to permit a greater sense of truth to life in acting and directing. Many of his detailed demands for a more natural acting style are similar to Ibsen's.

The change in theatre practice Ibsen wanted and clearly implied in the writing of his plays was achieved in Copenhagen in the early 1880s. In 1879, *A Doll's House* was directed by H. P. Holst in a traditional and convention-

ally accepted manner. The play was given two blocking
rehearsals, followed by eight general rehearsals and one
dress rehearsal. This was a pattern of work that relied upon
the individual inspiration and well-established routines of
star actors, rather than a pattern calculated to achieve any
kind of naturalist ensemble playing. Fittingly, it was the
acting of Betty Hennings as Nora that attracted the
attention of the critics. Despite some naturalist detail in the
setting, what the production offered was above all a
romantic tour de force from a gifted star actress (see Plate
1).

By 1883, William Bloch's production of *An Enemy of the
People* offered audiences a completely different kind of
experience, a fully thought-through naturalist production
in which a cohesive approach to set, costume and acting was
planned in meticulous detail and in which even the smallest
acting parts were thoroughly rehearsed. Bloch increased
the number of general rehearsals from eight to twenty and
concentrated the cast's attention on achieving a disciplined
ensemble style. In his promptbook, the crowd scene in Act
4 is annotated at such length that it required a separate
notebook to record the biographies and details of moves
and dialogue for each character in the mob.[2] The result was
detailed ensemble playing of a standard never before seen
in Scandinavia (see Plate 2).

Bloch went on to direct a whole series of Ibsen premières
at The Theatre Royal during the 1880s and 1890s,
establishing a naturalist theatre style in Scandinavia well
before its more general acceptance elsewhere in Europe.
Bloch never became an internationally well-known ad-
vocate of stage naturalism, partly because of reticence, and
partly because he was by nature a deeply conservative
individual who never shared the progressive and liberal
ideas of Ibsen and other naturalists. What he did share was

their concern for simplicity, naturalness and truth to life in the theatre. The real strength of his work lay in his respect for the hidden subtext in a play, what he called 'the hidden life of the soul', revealed on stage through gesture, intonation and moments of telling silence when actor and audience share some fleeting insight or emotion.

Later naturalist directors sometimes tended in their productions of Ibsen to pay too much attention to the physical environment on stage, swamping the stage with a surfeit of visual detail and neglecting in so doing the subtle inner life of the characters to which Bloch had paid so much attention. In Paris, Antoine mounted a production of *The Wild Duck* at the Théâtre Libre in 1891 that was full of authentic visual detail, but the production did not succeed in conveying the nuance and complexity of characterisation and symbolism in the play. The first-night audience quacked ironically at the production and Sarcey, one of Paris's leading critics, complained that the play was obscure, incoherent and insufferable (see Plate 3). Even the Moscow Arts Theatre was at times guilty of a similar imbalance in approach in its Ibsen productions with the stage so cluttered with furniture, curtains and knick-knacks that the characters were not so much shown to be determined by their environment (as Zola and Antoine had demanded in their theoretical work) as totally imprisoned within it.

A reaction against such naturalist excesses began as early as the 1890s, when a number of directors attempted to find a visual approach and an acting style that would do justice to the symbolism in Ibsen's mature plays. Lugné-Poë began this process with a production of *The Master Builder* in 1894. The stylised intonation of his actors and his pointed emphasis of the mysterious elements in the play were greeted with derision by cynical Parisian audiences. But he persevered undaunted and took his production on tour to Scandinavia. Ibsen met the director and his cast in Christiania and stressed that he was a passionate writer who needed to be acted with passion. According to Herman Bang, who was Lugné-Poë's Danish collaborator and adviser, Ibsen was deeply moved by the intensity of Lugné-Poë's acting.

Rather more esoteric experiments in symbolist approaches to Ibsen were to follow. In 1905, Meyerhold mounted his production of *Hedda Gabler* at Vera Komisarjevskaya's Dramatic Theatre in St Petersburg. It was a bold but drastic attempt to bring out the inner symbolism of the play by dispensing with all realistic detail. The stage was a shallow strip seen against a background of blues and autumnal gold: a large, vine-clad window with the blue sky beyond and an equally large tapestry in autumnal gold made up the major part of the background. The foreground was dominated by an armchair covered in white fur; the throne for 'a cold, regal, autumnal Hedda'. The acting was equally stylised, using a minimum of mime and gesture, relying on delicate eye movements and changes in facial expression and with widely spaced groupings on the broad but shallow stage.[3] The production was not well received.

In 1906, Gordon Craig directed an equally striking version of *Rosmersholm* in Florence, with Eleonora Duse as Rebecca. Duse was dressed in a long white sheath and Craig directed her to move like a spirit. The entire stage was given over to atmospheric effect, with long flowing drapes and a dominant central window opening out on to a misty beyond. Craig set out his view of the play in a programme note on the production:

The words are the words of actuality, but the drift of the words, something beyond this. There is the powerful impression of unseen forces closing in upon the place: we hear continually the long drawn out note of the horn of death. [. . .] Realism has long ago proclaimed itself as a contemptible means of hinting at things of life and death, the two subjects of the masters. Realism is only Exposure whereas art is Revelation; and therefore in the mounting of this play I have tried to avoid all Realism.[4]

Although Duse entered fully into the spirit of the production, the rest of the cast was uncertain how to respond to Craig's ideas. The result was an imbalanced and uneven production where the visual effects were more impressive than the acting[5] (see Plate 4).

A less spectacular but more convincing reinterpretation of an Ibsen play in a symbolist vein came from Max Reinhardt in 1906. Reinhardt wanted to open his newly built intimate theatre in Berlin, the Kammerspiele, with a production of *Ghosts* to mark Ibsen's death in May of that year. He invited the Norwegian artist Edvard Munch to provide design sketches for his production on the basis of detailed and meticulous notes he prepared in advance. In extending his invitation to Munch, he wrote: 'I am convinced that with your particular help we will be able to adjust the characters and the scenery to each other and to set them off in such a way, that we will illuminate as yet unfathomed depths in this splendid work . . .' His confidence was entirely justified. Munch's drawings brilliantly and expressively captured the mood and atmosphere of each act, showing figures isolated from each other in their anguish, within a visual setting dominated by oppressive colours and images: the walls a puce colour that reminded Reinhardt of the colour of rotting gums and a dominant black armchair in which Osvald finally collapses[6] (see Plate 5).

In his production, Reinhardt eschewed what he called 'the more or less successful clinical study of insanity' that had predominated in naturalist productions of the play by, for instance, August Lindberg in Sweden in 1883 and Otto Brahm at the Freie Bühne in Berlin in 1889. Instead, he concentrated on creating an atmosphere of sad resignation in a play that he saw above all as the tragedy of the mother. Agnes Sorma as Mrs Alving and Alexander Moissi as Osvald gave finely judged performances in this evocative reinterpretation of the play as a drama of suffering rather than a provocative drama of revolt.

Since Ibsen's death in 1906, his plays have been performed with increasing regularity all over the world. Productions in the inter-war years were mainly characterised by a series of outstanding acting performances (Edith Evans and Johanne Dybwad as Rebecca West (see Plate 6), Donald Wolfit as Solness, Gösta Ekman as Peer Gynt) rather than striking reinterpretations by gifted directors. (An exception was Gordon Craig's uncompromisingly symbolist version of *The Pretenders* at The Theatre Royal in Copenhagen in 1926, which deeply offended the well-established naturalist taste and sensibilities of Copenhagen's audiences.) After the cultural divide of the Second World War, a new generation of directors emerged in Europe, many of whom wrestled with the problem of finding as yet untried theatrical correlatives for Ibsen's dramatic vision. Some of the more recent approaches have been incisively original.

In 1964, for instance, Ingmar Bergman mounted a production of *Hedda Gabler* at the Royal Dramatic Theatre in Stockholm that was expressionist in its intensity. The set was stripped of unnecessary detail, the dull red and black colours of walls and furniture reflected Hedda's emotional confusion. A rehearsal screen divided the stage, allowing Gertrud Fridh as Hedda to react in mime to events on stage. The whole production was conceived as an extended exploration of Hedda's anguished state of mind, culminating in her suicide[7] (see Plate 7). (In 1970, Bergman was invited to direct his production with English actors for the Royal Shakespeare Company at the Aldwych Theatre in London. Maggie Smith as Hedda and John Moffatt as Brack exposed, with every glance and inflection of their voices, the ironic potential of the subtext, giving the production a more savagely comic quality than in Sweden where Gertrud Fridh had stressed Hedda's aristocratic distance from the world in which she found herself trapped (see Plate 8).) Bergman achieved a similar emotional intensity with his 1972 production of *The Wild Duck* in Stockholm. In this production, the upstage loft was transferred to a forestage area, allowing the audience to observe Hedvig's reactions to her father's thoughtlessly cruel rejection of her in the last act of the play. Max von Sydow, with his arms wrapped tightly around his body and his weight shifting uneasily from leg to leg, gave a memorable performance as Gregers Werle; every move he made was indecisive, clumsy, truncated, as he lived out his life in the shadow of his mother, whose portrait was seen in a dominant position in Act 1.

In England, Michael Elliott has established himself as a particularly sensitive Ibsen director, mounting the first full English production of *Brand* at the Lyric Opera House, Hammersmith in 1959 and productions of *Peer Gynt* for the London Old Vic in 1962 (with Leo McKern in the title role) and the 69 Theatre Company at Manchester in 1970 (with Tom Courtenay in the title role). In 1968 he directed an emotionally intense production of *When we dead awaken* (with Wendy Hiller as Irene and Alexander Knox as Rubek) and in 1978 a widely acclaimed production of

The Lady from the Sea. The production was initially mounted at The Royal Exchange Theatre in Manchester and later transferred to London. The set made effective and extensive use of water, constantly stressing the visual importance of water symbolism in the play. At its centre, the production had an impressive performance from Vanessa Redgrave as a deeply unhappy Ellida, torn by conflicting emotions within herself (see Plate 9).

Peter Hall at the National Theatre and John Barton at the Royal Shakespeare Company both contributed significant Ibsen reinterpretations during the 1970s. Peter Hall directed a restrained expressionist version of *John Gabriel Borkman* in 1975. The cast was flawless: Ralph Richardson as Borkman, Peggy Ashcroft as Ella Rentheim and Wendy Hiller as Gunhild. The set relied on visually effective emblems rather than distracting detail in order to reflect the spiritual state of mind of the protagonists. It shifted from the faded elegance of a sparsely furnished, grey-coloured interior in Act 1, to the cavernous emptiness of Borkman's room in Act 2 and finally to the icy grandeur of a snow-covered sloping revolve in the last act (see Plate 10).

John Barton's production of *Pillars of Society* at the Aldwych Theatre in 1977 brought out for the first time on stage the full ironic potential of the action and particularly the ending. Ian McKellan as Bernick and Judi Dench as Lona Hessel gave polished and intelligent performances within the ironic framework of the production. The setting was an opulently conceived garden room, the tableaux and atmosphere at times reminiscent of a Chekhov production, but the overall pace was deliberately fast. The illuminated ships seen through the windows in the last act were a fitting emblem for Bernick's extravagant aspirations. When the lights went out, his style was less flamboyant but his power no less real, as Ian McKellan's facial expressions clearly signalled to the audience (see Plate 11).

More recently, in the summer of 1982, the Royal Shakespeare Company presented yet another significant reinterpretation of an Ibsen play with Adrian Noble's production of *A Doll's House* at the newly opened Barbican Centre in London. Played in the round, with carefully chosen furniture and props, and casting Stephen Moore as Torvald and Cheryl Campbell as Nora, Adrian Noble showed London audiences the interactional dynamism of *A Doll's House* in an interpretation that stressed Torvald's potential for change. When Nora laid aside her extravagant effusiveness of the first two acts (an effusiveness that almost but never quite went over the top), Torvald was clearly prepared to listen to her in the final act and reflect seriously on the critique she had made of their relationship. Every nuance of feeling was conveyed in the facial expressions of the actors in a production that brilliantly exploited the proximity of actors and audience in a small studio theatre (see cover picture).

In West Berlin, the Marxist director Peter Stein presented a complex and provocative version of *Peer Gynt* at the Schaubühne am Halleschen Ufer in 1971. In a large functional set, encompassing the whole theatre, audiences were made to feel part of the action and were challenged to come to terms with what the director saw as the play's and their own bourgeois contradictions. The production was monumental, stretching over two evenings; the preparation was meticulous and the documentation gathered into a large book-format programme. Stein interpreted the play as an extended analysis of bourgeois individualism. The madhouse scene, for instance, in Act 4 was seen as an image of bourgeois selfishness in its most extreme form, the complete self-obsession of the lunatics being viewed as an extension of everyday bourgeois self-indulgence (see Plate 12). The final tableau, a pietà image of Peer curled up in Solvejg's lap, was shown as a consumerist image of Peer Gynt kitsch, illustrating in Solvejg's blind and deathly stare what Stein saw as the utter bankruptcy of bourgeois individualism (see Plate 13). The unstinting attention to detail in acting and staging made this one of Stein's most successful productions during the 1970s.[8]

If there is a common thread linking these various productions, it is this. Directors can today concentrate on the subtextual patterns of Ibsen's plays (or they can set out to comment on and elucidate the political or social assumptions behind his work) in the confident knowledge that actors on the modern stage are sufficiently versatile to express hidden or oblique insights through voice, body language, gesture, movement, blocking. (And here one thinks of how Ian McKellan's agile facial expressions showed Bernick's ability to think up new lies and subterfuges at lightning speed or how Cheryl Campbell expressed through movement, gesture and tone of voice Nora's growing hysteria at the crisis threatening her, culminating in the frenzied laughter and wild cartwheels she performed in the tarantella scene.)

In terms of staging, the naturalist bias of film and television has led to a general move away from naturalism on stage. Fully aware that the selective eye of the camera picks out significant detail far more effectively than an audience looking at a visually complex and distracting set, directors are no longer tempted to swamp their stage with too much visual detail. As a result, even Ibsen's ostensibly naturalist plays are normally staged in the modern theatre in a way that dispenses with fussy, naturalist detail in terms of set, furniture and costume. Instead, modern directors attempt to convey or comment on the kind of visual poetry to which Ibsen aspired by making use of significant colours, lighting and emblems in their stage setting and by ensuring that props, furniture and costume cohere in a way that is visually expressive.

What is the challenge that Ibsen presents to directors in the modern theatre? Part of the answer can be given in a descriptive account of modern productions. But an even more significant part may be sought in the play texts themselves. And here one must draw a distinction between the verse plays and the modern prose plays. In the verse plays, *Brand* and *Peer Gynt*, the poetry is the action. There are no aching gaps between the lines. Everything is stated. Situations and events provoke lengthy verbal comment and response. As in a play by Shakespeare, it is the way the poetry is phrased and pointed, the way it is framed by movement and visual effects, that conditions the audience's view of the play in production. In Ibsen's modern plays, by way of contrast, a world of meaning opens up between the lines.

Characters often fail to express in words their deepest feelings and communicate these with a look, a gesture, a tone of voice. The visual impact of the production is presupposed in the writing so that moves, tableaux, gestures, settings and lighting states are all written into the poetic fabric of the work. In these plays, it is the kinetic poetry of the stage that is the action and it is to that poetry that the audience is invited to respond.

The point may be illustrated by comparing a short scene from *Peer Gynt* with one from *Ghosts*. Towards the middle of Act V, Peer confronts a number of images of himself, culminating in a scene where he peels an onion in search of its innermost essence. The onion, like himself, is merely a series of layers and has no inner core. The verse is expansive and clearly expresses all of Peer's shifting moods. The whole scene builds towards a climax where Peer, an empty husk of a man who has never committed himself to anything or anyone, is confronted by a hut in the forest and the sight of Solvejg as a blind old woman. Again, the verse fully expresses Peer's feelings:

> One has remembered – and one has forgotten.
> One has squandered, and one has saved,
> O truth! And time can't be redeemed!
> O terror! Here's where my empire was!   [iii, p. 397]

Seemingly, there is little that can be added by a production to the clarity of the verse. Admittedly, the juxtaposition of Peer alone on stage peeling an onion and Peer confronted by a living image of Solvejg underscores visually the meaning of the verse. But that meaning is already fully expressed in the words. What can, however, be conveyed in production that is not specifically expressed in the words is a particular interpretation of Peer's responses. In this scene he can be shown to be a selfish aesthete confronted by a Kierkegaardian ethical imperative, or he can be shown as someone so psychologically immature that even here he still plays with words and concepts and runs from any responsibility, or, in a Marxist spirit, he can be shown as someone who resorts in his mind to bourgeois individualist solutions when under pressure. The director's task is to decide how the words are to be interpreted and then to find visual correlatives that match the interpretation.

In *Ghosts*, in Act 2, there is a decisive confrontation between Mrs Alving and Pastor Manders. At the end of it they relive a traumatic moment from their past, the moment when Mrs Alving had fled from her husband to Manders, only to be rejected by him:

MANDERS: Was it a crime to say to you: 'Woman, go back to your lawful husband'? When you came to me, demented, shouting: 'Here I am! Take me!' Was *that* a crime?

MRS ALVING: Yes, I think so.

MANDERS: We two don't understand each other.

MRS ALVING: Not any more, at least.

MANDERS: Never once . . . not in my most secret thoughts . . . have I ever regarded you as anything other than another man's wife.

MRS ALVING: You believe that?

MANDERS: Helene . . .

A world of feeling opens up between the lines here. The characters stand motionless, facing each other in the centre of the stage. Eye contact and facial expression help them to register even the most subtle motions of the soul. Manders, now as then, is evasive, unwilling to admit to feelings that he had communicated, however obliquely, to Mrs Alving before she left her husband. Indeed, he is so much on the defensive that Mrs Alving only has to make the most indirect of comments for him to deny any hint of emotional involvement. For her part, having once suffered the shame and hurt of his rejection and all that followed from it, she is determined to make him face up to the reality of what he felt and did. She dismisses his feeble attempt at self-justification and brings him face to face with the web of illusion and evasion on which his life is based. But all she actually says at the climactic moment is: 'You believe that?' The contempt in her voice and the ironic look in her eyes convey her real meaning. All Manders can do is articulate a cry of pain, asking perhaps for understanding, forgiveness, certainly mercy, a cry shaped around her name: 'Helene'. (And it is the only occasion in the play when he calls her by her Christian name.) Between the lines of the dialogue, as their eyes meet across a void of bitterness and misunderstanding, the whole relationship of Manders and Mrs Alving is conjured up, albeit fleetingly, its potential suggested, the waste clearly expressed at that moment when Manders rejected her and denied his own feelings. The actual words say very little. It is the acting that conveys the real meaning of the scene as these two characters face each other and express what they feel through intonation, facial expression and carefully restrained gesture.

There are many such examples of a minimalist approach, in terms of language, in Ibsen's mature plays, moments of intense emotion where the actors are expected to act out rather than state the essential meaning of a given scene. (The last few moments on stage of Rosmer and Rebecca are an outstanding example.) But at times, Ibsen demands the use of more flamboyant visual effects to convey to an audience the subtextual meaning of a scene. One of the most famous and beautifully written examples is the tarantella scene from *A Doll's House*. Nora is terrified that Torvald will find Krogstad's blackmailing letter if he goes to his letter box. She distracts his attention by playing the opening bars of the tarantella and asks his help in rehearsing the dance to prepare her for her performance at a fancy dress party the following day:

NORA (*shouts*): Now play for me! Now I'll dance! (*Helmer plays and Nora dances; Dr Rank stands at the piano behind Helmer and looks on.*)

HELMER (*playing*): Not so fast! Not so fast!

NORA: I can't help it.

HELMER: Not so wild, Nora!

NORA: This is how it has to be.

HELMER (*stops*): No, no, that won't do at all.

NORA (*laughs and swings the tambourine*): Didn't I tell you?

RANK: Let me play for her.

HELMER (*gets up*): Yes, do. Then I'll be better able to tell her what to do.

(*Rank sits down at the piano and plays. Nora dances more and more wildly. Helmer stands by the stove giving her repeated directions as she dances; she does not seem to hear them. Her hair comes undone and falls about her shoulders; she pays no attention and goes on dancing. Mrs Linde enters.*)

MRS LINDE (*standing as though spellbound in the door-way*): Ah . . . !   [v, pp. 258–9]

The dance itself is the most striking visual effect, a dance of death based on the agonised moves of those fatally wounded by the tarantula. Nora is seriously considering suicide, rather than let her husband suffer for her sake the shame of public scandal. She herself admits that she is dancing for her life, but the frenzy of her moves and her facial expression throughout the dance clearly express to an audience the anguish she feels inside her. Her role as a dancer also sums up the nature of her relationship with Torvald. She is a sexual object for her husband and she uses her status as a 'dancing girl' to buy attention and favours from him.

Rank says little during the scene. But his body language, the way he stands and looks at Nora as she dances, clearly indicates to an audience his depth of feeling for her. Unlike Torvald, he is not simply roused sexually by the sight of Nora: he would give anything, everything to serve her. His offer to play for her sums up that willingness. The image of Rank at the piano playing for his much loved Nora who is beyond his reach is poignantly expressive.

Mrs Linde enters as Nora's hair falls loose and her dance becomes more frenzied. Mrs Linde is spellbound and horrified by what she sees, by the way her friend has to dance in fancy dress and act out submissive sexual roles to achieve any kind of relationship with her husband. As she watches Nora, her facial expression communicates to an audience her resolve to intervene in Nora's marriage and make both Torvald and Nora confront the reality of their relationship.

Torvald, throughout the scene, is totally unaware of these subtextual feelings. His daily life is lived out at a brittle and shallow level. He never probes beyond the surface and takes people and events at face value. His responses are automatic and unthinking. In his view, his little wife is a rather wild creature who needs to be treated and trained like a child. On the other hand, he enjoys it when she is wild: it rouses him sexually. Her wildness gives him the excuse to assert his authority over her, which in turn confirms his sexual dominance. It simply never occurs to him to suspect that there are any hidden meanings, any hidden depths, in his wife's behaviour. His inability to see beyond a literal, surface impression is demonstrated in his posture, voice and facial expression. While the other three characters communicate subtextual emotions in their eyes, body language, moves, suggesting fleetingly a world of serious feeling beneath their social exterior, Torvald's shallow responses seem by comparison almost comically incongruous.

The kinetic poetry of the tarantella scene points clearly to the impending break between Torvald and Nora in Act 3. Characters who live out their lives at such totally different levels of response have no chance of understanding each other. The play leaves open the question as to whether Torvald will learn to think and respond with greater maturity and insight when he recovers from the shock of Nora's departure. The possibility is there. In the tarantella scene, however, the visual gulf between them is enormous. Nora dances a visually poetic statement of her frame of mind, expressing a complex and multi-layered view of life. Torvald struts around, full of his own self-importance, directing his wife in an unthinking parody of the rationalist autocrat whose view of life is stunted, simplistic, naïve.

Ibsen's mature work is full of such theatre poetry. To understand it properly, one must learn to read between the lines. One must also learn to read in visual images. The real significance of so many scenes is intended to be conveyed in moves, gestures, voice, body language, facial expression rather than in words. To flesh out this kinetic poetry, to give it form and substance, is the task of the director and the actors in an Ibsen production. The challenge facing them is to discover in their preparatory work what Ibsen himself called the poem hidden in the poem:

> For my song I have tuned my instrument low,
> but undertones give resonance to the music.
> Hence there is a poem hidden in the poem,
> and whoever understands *that* will understand my song.
>
> (Epic version of *Brand*)

Those directors and actors who successfully strike the deep and hidden resonances in Ibsen's work share with their audiences a poetic vision of human experience that is all the more precious for being revealed in fleeting moments of performance. That ultimately is what Ibsen's song is about.

7
The Response of Critics and Dramatists

Throughout his life, Ibsen often found his plays subjected to a barrage of hostile criticism when they were first published. This was as true of a poetic drama like *Peer Gynt* as of his more provocative social plays, such as *A Doll's House* and *Ghosts*. He occasionally expressed his irritation or fury at a particular critic's response in his letters, but never demeaned himself by replying to a critic in public. He was content to write for the future, confident that people would in time understand his work. He was also aware that he enjoyed enormous popularity and support amongst progressive young writers and theatre directors all over Europe, and during the 1880s and 1890s they rallied to his defence.

In England the key supporters of Ibsen in the theatre were the actress Janet Achurch, whose production of *A Doll's House* in 1889 caused a furore in London, and the Dutch journalist J. T. Grein who founded his Independent

Theatre in 1891 in order to present *Ghosts* to London audiences. The leading critical supporters of Ibsen were Edmund Gosse, William Archer and George Bernard Shaw. Gosse had tirelessly championed Ibsen's work in a series of essays published from the early 1870s onwards. Archer began publishing essays and translations from the 1880s. Shaw made a decisive contribution to the debate with his theatre criticism and his book *The Quintessence of Ibsenism* (1891), where he argued that Ibsen's plays were written, 'to illustrate his thesis that the real slavery of today is slavery to ideals of virtue'. Shaw saw Ibsen as a passionate moral reformer. His book may not have contributed greatly to an understanding of Ibsen as a poet, but it did help to undermine the arguments of conservative critics, such as Clement Scott writing for the *Daily Telegraph*, who had accused Ibsen of writing degrading, sensationalist filth.

Ibsen's work also had a decisive influence on Shaw's career as a playwright, inspiring him to write his early didactic plays revolving around social problems and moral issues. In *Widower's Houses* (1892) and *Mrs Warren's Profession* (1893) there was none of Ibsen's subtlety of characterisation nor his meticulous attention to structure; there was no resonant subtext for actors to bring alive in performance. But there was a biting wit and a polemic quickness of phrase that compensated for the artistic weaknesses of these early pieces. What Ibsen gave Shaw was the confidence to deal with even the most unmentionable social problems (from the point of view of Victorian society) in dramatic form, paving the way for him to find his own inimitable mode of blending thought and poetry in his later plays.

By the late 1890s, Ibsen's detractors all over Europe were largely silent and his supporters triumphantly welcomed his growing stature as a dramatist of international repute. In Scandinavia, his main critical supporters were Hans Jæger, Gerhard Gran and Georg Brandes. Brandes's book, *Henrik Ibsen, a critical study* (first published in 1899 but reprinted in 1964), is still an eminently readable account of Ibsen's work from a progressive naturalist perspective. The same is true of Otto Brahm's essay on Ibsen, first published in 1886 and reprinted in a collection of essays on Ibsen, edited by Fritz Paul in his book, *Henrik Ibsen* (1977). Brahm, as a critic and the founder of Germany's first independent theatre, the Freie Bühne, played a crucial role in bringing Ibsen's plays to the attention of German readers and audiences. (The Freie Bühne began its activities with a production of *Ghosts* in 1889.)

The impact of Ibsen's plays on German writers was substantial, particularly in the case of the young Gerhart Hauptmann. His first play, *Before Sunrise* (*Vor Sonnenaufgang*, 1889) a naturalist melodrama containing a number of echoes from Ibsen's work in terms of theme and characterisation, was followed by a play with a rich emotional subtext called *Lonely Lives* (*Einsame Menschen*, 1891). The central relationship in the play is modelled closely on *Rosmersholm*, as Hauptmann explores a reality of feeling that cannot adequately be conveyed in words but only in symbolic or destructive gestures.

Ibsen's influence was felt even in the strictly censored theatre world of Tzarist Russia. Not only did leading young directors mount productions of his work, but Chekhov also responded to the impact of Ibsen's plays, although at times almost resentfully. In many ways Chekhov's approach as a dramatist was diametrically opposed to that of Ibsen. In his mature work he strove to capture the passing moment, and it was a moment in Russian history when a particular culture was dying. In *The Three Sisters* (1901) and *The Cherry Orchard* (1904), he shows characters trapped by their upbringing, their prejudices and their environment. In contrast to Ibsen, Chekhov showed his characters as seemingly incapable of making responsible choices, the odds against them appear too overwhelming. Hence the emphasis in his plays on a wistful or ironic portrayal of character rather than the tracing out of action. All of this is far removed from Ibsen's resolute commitment to the notion of human freedom and agency. And yet there are parallels in the work of the two writers.

In all his mature plays, and particularly in *The Seagull* (1896), Chekhov follows Ibsen's example of using visual and verbal symbols to add resonance to the action and to explore facets of a given character's response, for instance the revealing contrast in Lopakhin's and Mrs Ranevsky's view of the cherry orchard, or the widely differing attitudes of the major characters to the seagull. Chekhov also develops Ibsen's pioneering use of a richly woven subtext to the point where the actual words spoken in some of his scenes seem quite inconsequential or incongruous. It is the actors' task to show, not state, the actual meaning of such scenes. Chekhov quite brilliantly adapted Ibsen's techniques to serve his own very different needs and aspirations as a writer.

Ibsen's impact on later writers has varied from openly acknowledged admiration – as in the case of Arthur Miller, whose two outstanding social plays, *All my Sons* (1947) and *Death of a Salesman* (1949), owe a clear thematic debt to Ibsen's work – to a grudging recognition by a Marxist writer such as Brecht that Ibsen's plays are 'important historical documents' although 'a modern spectator can't learn anything from them'.[1] Even in Brecht's case, however, there are important points of contact between his mature work and Ibsen's. In plays like *Galileo* (1937–9) and *Mother Courage* (1938–9), Brecht attempted, as Ibsen had done in his social plays, to place the sufferings and shortcomings of individuals in their historical context and in that way to explain and illuminate them.

Turning to modern writers, Ibsen's importance for Pinter, despite their divergent views on human nature, has already been mentioned.[2] But the contemporary playwright whose vision is closest to Ibsen's is Edward Bond. Both share a passionate belief in human freedom and dignity: both see man ultimately as the agent of his own fate. In his work, Bond has taken inspiration from a wide variety of sources, but in *The Sea* (1973) and in his latest play *Summer* (1982), he uses a number of techniques that are reminiscent of Ibsen's mature work; evocative visual and verbal symbolism, a densely woven poetic subtext and the structural archetype of a friend or relative arriving in order to spark off the action. Even his use of ironic juxtaposition of response in these two plays (for instance, the hectoring and domineering Mrs Rafi contrasted with the thoughtfully observant Willy Carson in *The Sea*) is reminiscent of Ibsen's use of ironically contrasted responses, as in the case of Bernick and Lona Hessel or Torvald and Nora.

Critical responses to Ibsen have grown in volume and variety throughout the twentieth century. In the 1920s and 1930s, critics centred their attention on an extrinsic approach. Ibsen's plays were rarely discussed as poetic statements in their own right, but were viewed in relation to his life or the philosophical and psychological assumptions of his age. A number of studies also discussed his work in the light of psychoanalytic thought. Hermann Weigand's Freudian account of the prose plays in *The Modern Ibsen* (first published in 1925 but reprinted in 1970) is an outstanding example.

After the Second World War, the dominant critical focus shifted to an intrinsic, analytic approach, inspired by the principles of New Criticism. The job of the critic, as F. R. Leavis defined it in *The Common Pursuit* was, 'to ensure relevance of response and to determine what is actually *there* in the work of art'. That task was undertaken in respect of Ibsen by a number of post-war English critics. Muriel Bradbrook, in *Ibsen the Norwegian* (1946), and Raymond Williams, in *Drama from Ibsen to Eliot* (1952), wrote sympathetic accounts of Ibsen's plays, based on subjective response, sensitive intuition and an analytic feel for linguistic and structural patterns. P. F. D. Tennant's *Ibsen's Dramatic Technique* (1948), and John Northam's *Ibsen's Dramatic Method* (1953), opened up fruitful avenues of insight into Ibsen's use of theatrical symbolism and effects, visual suggestion and parallel situations in his plays. John Northam made particularly effective use of Ibsen's draft material in determining the significance of what was actually *there* in his finished plays.

In Norway, a New Critical approach has predominated in the work of Daniel Haakonsen. In his book, *Henrik Ibsens realisme* (1957), he used a combination of close analysis and subjective intuition to argue that Ibsen, in his plays, had created 'a kind of tragedy of fate adapted to our time'. Haakonsen's latest book on Ibsen, a profusely and beautifully illustrated volume entitled *Henrik Ibsen. Mennesket og kunstneren* (*Henrik Ibsen. The Man and the Artist*, 1981), is a thematically based study of the plays, though with a strong biographical slant in certain chapters and some of the illustrations. Else Høst's impressively detailed monographs on *Hedda Gabler* (1958) and *Vildanden av Henrik Ibsen* (*The Wild Duck by Henrik Ibsen*, 1967) while admitting a biographical perspective, are nevertheless firmly rooted in the New Critical tradition of close textual analysis in terms of imagery, theme and structure.

Recent studies in the USA have tended to concentrate on the 'deep structures' that critics have discerned in Ibsen's work. James Hurt, for instance, in his book, *Catiline's Dream* (1972), argues that a consistent mythic pattern, with schizoid overtones, can be traced in all of Ibsen's plays: 'The Ibsen protagonist, terrified by a threatening and bewildering outer world, divided against himself, and retreating into obsessive projects of the will, is a remarkably accurate representation of modern man himself' (p. 204). Charles Lyons in *Henrik Ibsen: the Divided Consciousness* (1972), argues that the primary concern of Ibsen in his various plays 'is an exploration of the mythological functions of consciousness which attempts to create an image of selfhood and his recognition of the failure of that process' (p. xxix). More recently, Errol Durbach, in *Ibsen the Romantic* (1982), has attempted to chart the essentially romantic quest he sees at the heart of all of Ibsen's work, a quest located in 'a drama of spiritual distress, in his protagonists' search for consolation in the face of death, and their attempt to rediscover a world of lost Paradisal hopes in the mythology of Romanticism' (pp. 6–7).

Diametrically and polemically opposed to the work of the New Critics and the Structuralists are the Marxist critics of post-war Europe. Some, for instance the Swedish theatre critic and director Göran Eriksson, have been inclined to view Ibsen disparagingly as an author who exemplified and reflected in his work the paradoxes and inconsistencies at the heart of bourgeois liberalism. Others, notably Horst Bien in his book *Henrik Ibsens Realismus* (1970), have seen Ibsen as an impassioned opponent of bourgeois society who came to feel that bourgeois attitudes and life styles were so stiflingly inhuman that they needed to be destroyed root and branch. Bien regards Ibsen's social plays as his masterpieces, with resourceful protagonists firmly rooted in a specific social environment. The protagonists of the later plays he criticises as 'morbid or sickly, unable or unwilling to establish any meaningful relationship to their environment' (p. 250). As he sees it, the late plays reflect the crisis of a bourgeois society in decline.

Ibsen's work is clearly of sufficient stature and complexity to inspire successive generations of critics to find new perspectives on his plays. And that process will certainly continue. If it is nevertheless true, as Ronald Gray claims in his polemically argued book, *Ibsen – a Dissenting View* (1977), that the case for Ibsen as a poet has still to be made, then the substance of that case will lie in elucidating the kinetic poetry at the heart of Ibsen's mature plays. Ibsen's vision of the poetry of experience was a dynamic one, which was why he wrote plays and not novels, why he suggested and hinted obliquely at shifts of mood and response rather than stated, fixed and analysed his characters. His area of concern as a poet was that whole elusive area of the 'between', the relationship between the characters in his plays and between them and their society, the dialectical relationship presupposed between actors and audience. These relationships constantly shift as the actions of his plays develop. The task of audiences and critics is to note and respond to the shifting patterns in each work and to appreciate the significance of one pattern juxtaposed with another – a word undercut by a glance, a purely visual response by one character to a move or statement of another, a loving phrase delivered in the context of emotional pressure, a claim of the ideal tainted by environmental conditioning, an unthinking surface response contrasted with a response rich in subtextual insight. This is the stuff and substance of Ibsen's theatre poetry.

Ibsen chose the miner's hammer as his personal symbol, and the significance of this is quite clear when one recalls the couplet from his poem, *The Miner*:

> Bryd mig vejen, tunge hammer,
> til det dulgtes hjertekammer!
>
> Break my way then, heavy hammer
> To life's innermost secret chamber.

The task he set himself as a writer was to pierce through words and appearances, the surface rhetoric of drama and the superficial skin of external reality, to a deeper level of meaning and understanding. In the kinetic poetry of his mature plays, a poetry that presupposes the thoughtful and subtle realisation of his work on stage, Ibsen opened up a route into life's 'innermost secret chamber', into the hidden vaults of the heart and mind. His conviction that actors, audiences and critics would be able to follow him along that route was the resolute premise on which he based his work as a poet of the theatre. 'Only connect . . .' That is the invitation he extends every time we watch or read one of his plays.

References

1. Life and Work

1. Bergliot Ibsen, *The Three Ibsens* (London: Hutchinson, 1951), p. 12.
2. Letter to Frederik Hegel, his publisher, 12 July 1871.
3. Letter to the actress Lucie Wolf, 25 May 1883, quoted from J. McFarlane (ed.), *Henrik Ibsen. A Critical Anthology* (Penguin Books, 1970) p. 102.
4. See Einar Østvedt, *Henrik Ibsen and the Surroundings of his Childhood* (Skien: Ibsenforbundet, 1977).

2. Literary and Theatrical Influences

1. For a thorough and detailed analysis of an early Ibsen promptbook at Bergen, see R. Rudler, 'Ibsens debut som sceneinstruktør' in *Ibsenårbok 1960–62* (Skien, 1962), pp. 46–81.
2. See Rudler, p. 73 and Halvdan Koht, *The Life of Ibsen*. Vol. 1 (London: Allen & Unwin, 1931), p. 87.
3. See Rudler, p. 73.

References

3. Philosophical and Aesthetic Ideas

1. See J. Macquarrie, *Existentialism* (London : Pelican Books, 1973), p. 210.
2. *Hegel on Tragedy*, edited by Anne and Henry Paolucci (New York: Harper & Row, 1975), p. 132.
3. Georg Brandes, *Henrik Ibsen. A Critical Study* (1899) (reprinted New York: Benjamin Blom, 1964), p. 53.

4. Dolls' Houses

1. See Hans Kleven, *Klassestrukturen i det norske samfunnet* (Oslo: Forlaget, Ny Dag, 1965), pp. 30–3.
2. Kleven, p. 74.
3. See J. W. McFarlane, 'Meaning and evidence in Ibsen's drama' in Daniel Haakonsen (ed.), *Contemporary Approaches to Ibsen*, Vol. 1 (Oslo: Universitetsforlaget, 1966), pp. 35–50.
4. In 1848 there was only one commercial banking firm in Christiania, by 1875 there were eleven. See Kleven, pp. 61–4.
5. John Northam was the first to point this out in his book, *Ibsen's Dramatic Method* (London: Faber, 1953), pp. 15–38.
6. Letter to the Danish newspaper *Nationaltidende*, 20 February 1880 [v, p. 454].
7. See David Thomas, 'Patterns of interaction in Ibsen's *Ghosts*', in *Ibsenårbok* (Oslo: Universitetsforlaget, 1974), pp. 89–117.
8. David Hare, 'A lecture' in *Licking Hitler* (London: Faber, 1978), p. 69.
9. Letter to Count Moritz Prozor, 4 December 1890.

5. Symbolist Plays

1. Sigmund Freud, 'Some character-types met with in psychoanalytical work' (1916), reprinted in James McFarlane (ed.), *Henrik Ibsen. A Critical Anthology* (London: Penguin Books, 1970), pp. 392–9.
2. For a detailed account of the various classical and Christian references in the action, see David Thomas, 'All the glory of the world: reality and myth in *When we dead awaken*', in *Scandinavica* (1979), 18, pp. 1–19.
3. Letter to Bjørn Kristensen, 13 February 1887.

References

6. Ibsen in Production

1. The original letters are reprinted in Øyvind Anker (ed.), *Henrik Ibsens brevveksling med Christiania Theater, 1878–99* (Oslo, 1965).

2. For more detailed accounts of Bloch's production, see F. J. and L. L. Marker, *The Scandinavian Theatre* (Oxford: Blackwell, 1975), pp. 166–71; and Kela Kvam, 'William Bloch og Ibsen' in J. Wiingaard (ed.), *Henrik Ibsen i scenisk belysning* (København, 1978), pp. 49–99.

3. A detailed account of the production can be found in Edward Braun, *The Director and the Stage* (London: Methuen, 1982), pp. 59–63.

4. Gordon Craig, *A Note on Rosmersholm*, December 1906 (British Museum).

5. See Edward Craig, *Gordon Craig. The Story of his Life* (London, 1968), pp. 217–20.

6. A full account of Reinhardt's and Munch's collaboration can be found in Hans Midbøe, *Max Reinhardts iscenesettelse av Ibsens Gespenster i Kammerspiele des Deutschen Theaters, Berlin 1906* (Trondheim, 1969).

7. A more detailed account of Bergman's approach to the play can be found in L. L. and F. J. Marker: *Ingmar Bergman. Four Decades in the Theater* (Cambridge University Press, 1982), pp. 178–201 and in Henrik Sjögren, *Ingmar Bergman på teatern* (Stockholm, 1968), pp. 253–63.

8. A detailed account of Stein's approach may be found in Michael Patterson, *Peter Stein* (Cambridge University Press, 1982), pp. 66–89.

7. The Response of Critics and Dramatists

1. *Brecht on Theatre*, edited and translated by John Willet (London: Methuen, 1978), p. 66.

2. See p. 135 above.

Select Bibliography

1. Standard Editions of the Plays

Samlede verker, hundreårsutgave (centenary edition). 22 vols. Edited by Halvdan Koht, Francis Bull and Didrik Arup Seip (Oslo: Gyldendal, 1928–58).
The Oxford Ibsen. 8 vols. Edited by James McFarlane (Oxford University Press, 1960–77).

2. Biographical Studies

Halvdan Koht, *The Life of Ibsen*. 2 vols (London: Allen & Unwin, 1931).
Michael Meyer, *Ibsen* (Penguin Books, 1974).

3. Late Nineteenth- and early Twentieth-century Criticism

Georg Brandes, *Henrik Ibsen. A Critical Study* (1899) (New York: Benjamin Blom, 1964).
Michael Egan (ed.), *Ibsen: the Critical Heritage* (London: Routledge & Kegan Paul, 1972).

169

Select Bibliography

George Bernard Shaw, *The Quintessence of Ibsenism* (London: Walter Scott, 1891).

H. J. Weigand, *The Modern Ibsen: a Reconsideration* (1925) (Freeport, NY: Books for Libraries Press, 1970).

4. New Critical Studies

M. C. Bradbrook, *Ibsen the Norwegian: a Revaluation* (1946) (London: Chatto and Windus, 1966).

Francis Fergusson, *The Idea of a Theater* (Princeton University Press, 1949).

Daniel Haakonsen, *Henrik Ibsens realisme* (Oslo, 1957).

Daniel Haakonsen, *Henrik Ibsen. Mennesket og kunstneren* (Oslo, 1981).

Else Høst, *Hedda Gabler. En monografi* (Oslo: Aschehoug, 1958).

Else Høst, *Vildanden av Henrik Ibsen* (Oslo: Aschehoug, 1967).

John Northam, *Ibsen's Dramatic Method: a Study of the Prose Dramas* (1953) (Oslo: Universitetsforlaget, 1971).

John Northam, *Ibsen. A Critical Study* (Cambridge University Press, 1973).

P. F. D. Tennant, *Ibsen's Dramatic Technique* (Cambridge: Bowes & Bowes, 1948).

Raymond Williams: *Drama from Ibsen to Eliot* (1952) (Peregrine Books, 1964).

5. Historical Criticism and Literary History

Edvard Beyer, *Ibsen: the Man and his Work* (London: Souvenir Press, 1978).

Brian Downs, *Ibsen. The Intellectual Background* (Cambridge University Press, 1948).

James McFarlane, *Ibsen and the Temper of Norwegian Literature* (Oxford University Press, 1960).

Maurice Valency, *The Flower and the Castle. An Introduction to Modern Drama* (London: Macmillan, 1963).

6. Marxist and Structuralist Studies

Horst Bien, *Henrik Ibsens Realismus* (Berlin: Rütten & Loenig, 1970).

Errol Durbach, *Ibsen the Romantic* (London: Macmillan, 1982).

Select Bibliography

Orley Holtan, *Mythic Patterns in Ibsen's Last Plays* (University of Minnesota Press, 1970).

James Hurt, *Catiline's Dream: an Essay on Ibsen's Plays* (University of Illinois Press, 1972).

Charles Lyons, *Henrik Ibsen. The Divided Consciousness* (Southern Illinois University Press, 1972).

7. Theatre History

Øyvind Anker (ed.), *Henrik Ibsens brevveksling med Christiania Theater, 1878–99* (Oslo, 1965).

F. J. and L. L. Marker, *The Scandinavian Theatre. A Short History* (Oxford: Blackwell, 1975).

Hans Midbøe, *Max Reinhardts iscenesettelse av Ibsens Gespenster i Kammerspiele des Deutschen Theaters Berlin 1906* (Trondheim, 1969).

8. Collections of Essays

Errol Durbach (ed.), *Ibsen and the Theatre* (London: Macmillan, 1980).

Rolf Fjelde (ed.), *Ibsen. A Collection of Critical Essays* (Englewood Cliffs, NJ: Prentice-Hall, 1965).

Daniel Haakonsen (ed.), *Contemporary Approaches to Ibsen*. 4 vols (Oslo: Universitetsforlaget, 1966–79).

James McFarlane (ed.), *Henrik Ibsen. A Critical Anthology* (Penguin Books, 1970).

Fritz Paul (ed.), *Henrik Ibsen* (Darmstadt: Wissenschaftliche Buchgesellschaft, 1977).

Index

For the convenience of readers not familiar with Scandinavian alphabets, the letters å and æ have been listed under a, ö and ø under o. Titles of plays and critical works are listed under the name of the appropriate author.

Index

Index

Index

Index